babyopathy

Relaxed Mum, Contented Baby!

Including
**the Routine
in the Womb**
campaign

Angela J Spencer

babyopathy
Relaxed Mum, Contented Baby!

First published in 2014
Second Edition published in 2019 by

Panoma Press Ltd
48 St Vincent Drive, St Albans, Herts, AL1 5SJ, UK
info@panomapress.com
www.panomapress.com

Book layout by Michael Inns
Artwork by Karen Gladwell

ISBN 978-1-784521-27-1

This book is available online and in bookstores.

Dedication

For my amazing children who I love completely and without whom I would not have begun my research.

For my wonderful parents without whom I would not have been inspired to open my first nursery or make it through the sleepless nights.

For the thousands of children, families and staff that passed through my care during 25 years of owning nurseries, you were my life's work.

And for the pregnant mums and their babies I now work with, you are my continued passion.

Book Reviews and Testimonials

Hertfordshire GP – Dr David Maddams

Review: Love the Babyopathy concept and its positive energy. A nice, original if not fascinating idea – it grabs you (or did me!). The sensory section could cause a 'revolution' in how we nurture our babies before and after birth.

Testimonial: *Angela has drawn on her huge experience of childcare to produce a unique book to get everyone thinking from mums and dads to professionals and policy makers.*

Psychotherapist, Counsellor & Easy-Birthing Practitioner – Natasha Crowe

Review: I enjoyed the book, I liked the tone, it was friendly and I didn't feel patronised, which can often be the case with baby or parenting books.

Testimonial: *A book that supports parents in using their intuition by helping them to enjoy their parenting journey.*

Mother of one – Sarah

Review: Love it! If only this had been around when I had my son! Clearly written by someone who has had both professional and personal experience of baby care and is not afraid to say 'keep it simple'.

Testimonial: *What new mums need is simple, straightforward honesty which is what is in this book.*

Mother of two (three years and eight weeks) – Lucy

Review: For a busy mum of two, I thought it was easy to read with the limited time I have. I liked the Top Tips and Crystal notes to use. I liked the Breastfeeding section the most as although I have breastfed both of mine this was a good approach. There is far too much pressure to breastfeed by midwives etc.

Testimonial: *Refreshingly realistic. I wish I had this book when I had my first child!*

Acknowledgements

So, the little blue line appeared in the
second window, congratulations!

Now is the start of an amazing journey
and so this book is for you…

CONTENTS

Chapter One

What is Babyopathy?

babyopathy

Relaxed Mum, Contented Baby!

What is Babyopathy?

Babyopathy is 'baby led sensory development' ... but what exactly does that mean?

Give a baby an experience and they will want to know more!

If a baby is just left in a cot with no interaction or sensory stimulation, what do you think they will learn? How do you think they will develop? Well I can tell you they will follow a certain natural developmental path as time passes but that development will most likely be slower and stunted in many ways.

If, however, you nurture and stimulate their senses from the moment they begin to develop and give them a world of interaction and experiences, how do you think they will develop then? What do you think they will learn?

The answer this time is 'anything and everything' is possible!

However, for some reason beyond my comprehension we are 'leaving' babies to their own devices – but this time, literally! It has become normal to put a baby in front of a screen or for us to be glued to it instead and so therefore human interaction is at its all-time low for these beautiful babies. Research proves a lack of interaction with babies severely affects their social and emotional well-being and natural development – put them in front of a screen too and you throw in stunted physical development, speech delays, lack of cognitive skills and behavioural problems – fact, not fiction!

However, the more you interact with your baby, the more experiences you give them, the more they will want. Their brain will naturally begin to look for the interaction, look for more experiences and do their very best to respond, even from within the womb. If you also give them a sensory routine to follow, allow their senses to recognise what 'time' of the day it is (nap time, milk time or play time) they will also naturally find their own rhythm in the world that naturally nurtures their well-being and development. But they will also be much more contented!

Babyopathy gives you those tools to nurture your baby's natural sensory journey from where it starts, in the womb, and thus nurture their whole well-being too. It gives you the knowledge that we seem to have lost over the years to support your baby's unique developmental path, and it supports your journey as a mum in today's busy and stressful world - and that begins before you even become pregnant!

So now you know what Babyopathy is, here are our passions when it comes to what we do; we hope that you find and believe in these passions too…

babyopathy is committing to the health and sensory well-being for the expectant mother and her baby

babyopathy is loving yourself as you are and trusting yourself and your judgment

babyopathy is empowering parents to embrace their baby's sensory journey through pregnancy, birth and beyond

babyopathy means no judgment, just support, self-belief and knowledge with toolkits to support your choices with no guilt, whilst meeting mental health head on – talking, feeling you can't cope or asking for support is not a failure, it's being a Super Hero Mum!

There are so many 'How to' books for bringing up baby or weaning your baby etc. so you probably think this is just another one! However, this baby book isn't a new fad, it isn't a poorly thought through regime that you and your baby will struggle to follow and it isn't out to scaremonger (although I will give you facts). It is a mix of my experiences that led me to begin my research on sensory development and the human-nature connection and subsequently to introduce the Babyopathy (and Nascuropathy – for our children over one year) programmes into my nurseries. It is an insight into how you can use the programme at home and also all of the advice I could think of that may help support you and your baby during your first year. Most of all though, I hope it brings you comfort to know you are not alone, you are doing great and there is someone who understands.

Parenthood should be about doing the best for you and your baby that **you** can. It is not about doing everything, not everything suits everyone. However, if I can give you as much information as I can or as many hints and tips that I have picked up along the way then hopefully you will find your own way to be a Super Hero for your baby. I do love a Super Hero reference and after all, just like mums, Super Heroes come in all different shapes and sizes with their own style of super power – be your own style of Super Hero! Most of all, the message is to relax. Because a relaxed mum means your baby will not be stressed and so relaxed and contented too, then everything happens naturally.

The human-nature connection

I have purposely written this book so that it isn't technical or overpowering (I hope), but I feel it is important that you understand one of the main core theories behind the programmes and that is the human-nature connection.

Whilst the theory has been around for many decades, Edward O Wilson, American biologist and researcher in Sociobiology, coined the phrase 'Biophilia' for his 1984 book *The Biophilia Hypothosis*. The hypothesis describes the connection that human beings subconsciously have with the rest of life and proposed the possibility that the deep affiliations humans have with nature are rooted in our biology.

This hypothesis was further researched by Stephen R Kellert, Professor Emeritus at Yale University, in which he explored the importance of childhood contact with nature, and *"particularly for children's emotional, intellectual and evaluative development and how their physical and mental well-being depends on the quality of their experience of the natural world."*

Through his research, Stephen R Kellert concludes that children experience nature in three different levels of contact:

Direct – Indirect – Vicarius

To help you understand the difference:

Direct contact is when a child experiences nature spontaneously without other human initiation or control, such as free exploration of a back garden where they are free to climb trees, get muddy and wet or catch things like bugs!

Indirect contact is when a child's interaction with nature depends on ongoing human intervention or management and tends to be planned or structured such as in zoos or botanical gardens or with domesticated pets. Contact cannot be spontaneous and experiences are limited.

Vicarious or symbolic contact does not involve the child having any actual contact with nature but rather with images or representation that includes natural materials, shapes and designs.

In today's society, children's nature experiences are mostly limited to indirect opportunities to interact with nature. For many, nature is represented by garden or house plants and domesticated animals but what children now desperately need to include are habitats such as forests and meadows as well as the weather and broader spectrum of animals. Unfortunately, direct interaction, the most important and influential, is extremely restricted in recent years especially due to the impact of society development and technology.

The conclusion of my research, and my evolution of the biophilia hypothesis, is that in today's built-up environments and technological influences it is vital that first and foremost a vicarious environment is created to nurture the biophilia hypothesis and in turn natural development, and where possible it is imperative to provide additional opportunity for direct and indirect nature interaction. However, it is not just nature as described by Stephen R Kellert that we need to be connected to, it is all life, human life connections too.

Babies and children are so disconnected now due to the social and technological influences (amongst others) that it is causing the appearance of mental health concerns, widening developmental delays and putting an entire generation at risk. This is evidenced in the pregnancy and birth experiences, including the alarming rise of miscarriage, stillbirth and neonatal death. The continued rise of post-natal depression is leaving many mums feeling disconnected from their baby and family, resulting in a baby's disconnection from an early age.

The use of computer/mobile phone screens by many mums, whether given to their baby or using them themselves, is disconnecting mums from their babies at a crucial time for both. Living our lives through social media and a screen results in being truly disconnected from our babies and children. The lack of supportive and positive care for many during their pregnancy, birth and first years is also contributing to a mum being disconnected. Women thrive on the connection and support of other women and today's society contradicts this in its behaviour.

In order to support both the biophilia hypothesis and my extensive research into the sensory stimulation concept I developed two programmes:

> **Babyopathy** – that nurtures and supports the sensory journey beginning in the womb through the first year of life in a sensory and vicarious natural environment, activities and resources.

> **Nascuropathy** – that nurtures and supports natural and progressive child development and adult lifestyle, through a sensory and biophilic environment, activities and resources from age one to 100 (and beyond!).

Many programmes take one theory to the extreme such as Forest or Nature schools and sensory only programmes. Whilst individually their focuses have benefits, like anything in life, lifestyles or education programmes that are too extreme or too focused on one aspect have their own extreme limitations too and do not reflect modern, everyday life and experiences, leading to a danger of children not being able to integrate into future life scenarios.

Where both Babyopathy and Nascuropathy are different though is ensuring a balance between natural world interaction, sensory stimulation through my toolkits and everyday life and routines.

The Babyopathy way

OK so, enough of the technical, mind-bending bit for now! Having a baby should not be about having to conform to some military like regime and it should not be a time of guilt or added stress. Having a baby should be something natural that makes your family complete and, let's face it, people have been having babies for millennia so by now it should be easy and stress free, right?

Wrong! For so many new mums I speak to that's not always the case, and according to a report commissioned by Nurofen for Children published in January 2014, the average first-time mum doesn't fully enjoy motherhood until the baby is six months old, with one in six mums saying they didn't really enjoy their baby until they had passed their first birthday. In this report, new mums admitted they were baffled with many aspects of motherhood including health, illness, feeding and safety. The study found 52% of mothers felt like they had lost their identity after having a child and 35% missed being able to leave the house. NB: This is an updated version of my original book and statistics have not improved.

In my opinion one of the factors that has contributed to mums feeling this way is the constant pressure they face every time some new fad is published that they feel they should follow because it states it is 'the new and best way to bring up your baby'. Other baby and child 'programmes and teachings' promote a regimented practice that quite often results in extremely stressed parents and babies, or a free will attitude with no boundaries and no stimulation resulting in parents unable to control their children and children with no self-control.

We don't live in the same community structures we did 25 years ago, and many don't have their mum close by for various reasons who would have passed on their own knowledge and helped to care for you and the baby in those early weeks. This is why I created Mentor Mums which you can read about later.

None of these regimes are ensuring a healthy balance of child/ adult initiated experiences or routines with freedom of expression and individuality or most importantly, sufficient support and reassurance to parents.

My main driving force for originally researching and developing the Babyopathy programme many years ago was because as a new mum I felt let down by the lack of reliable and valid information and support and yet I was lucky enough to have my own mother close by and the knowledge I had gained from my time as owner of the nurseries. I wanted that to change for the babies and families I was responsible for.

Babyopathy comes from my own 25 years of research and expertise in the childcare profession; it takes you back to basics the way nature intended. It gives you the sensory tools and knowledge of how to ensure your baby has the best start in life and how to enhance your family environment.

It is a nature and sensory based lifestyle programme for you and your baby that is vital to the natural development of your baby and the harmonious home life for you and your family. In addition, it is good, back to basics, common sensed advice that you *need* to know.

Babyopathy is therefore completely unique! It is the *only* baby care and development programme to encompass both all-round sensory stimulation and the human-nature connection. Babyopathy aims to help you be a relaxed mum with a contented baby!

Mother Nature – it's not just an old-fashioned term

The inspiration behind Babyopathy is the natural worlds around us. Nature supplies us with everything we need as a basis to survive and develop and has given us our senses to guide us along the way. From the air that we breathe to water to quench our thirst, Mother Nature provides it all – if we don't continually destroy it! If we stop and look, nature not only provides us with the food and water our bodies need but has also created a sensory oasis to nurture our spiritual and emotional well-being.

To give you an example, imagine you are sitting in a meadow full of wildflowers on a beautiful sunny day. The image you see before your eyes is indeed a beautiful one created by nature and is instantly relaxing. However, if you just stop for a moment and close your eyes, the rest of your senses will be bombarded with sensory information to almost instantly give you an instinctual feeling of calm and serenity… the warmth of the sun on your skin, the smell of the wildflowers that surround you, the buzzing of the insects and sounds of the birds and the colour of the sun through your eyes.

Nature is teaching you to observe, learn and benefit without you even realising, it is giving you the tools that you need to deal with the stresses of life and to bring you comfort. So, it follows that from the moment a baby's senses begin to develop their senses take over and from the moment of birth begin to guide them on their journey.

Babyopathy uses everything nature has to offer that can enhance and nurture your baby's natural development; it shows you how to create perfect nature and sensory environments using natural imagery, aromatherapy, music and sound and colour, setting the scene for you and your baby to bond and grow together naturally. By following the whole Babyopathy programme you are giving your baby a natural, sensory start to their journey through life to naturally reach their full potential.

The Babyopathy Toolkits

Throughout every stage of your pregnancy, from pre-conception through to the birth and beyond, I will give you a sensory based toolkit, as well as other hints and tips, to help you get through each stage feeling like a Super Hero rather than a 'parenting fail' video candidate – I can say that as I've been there! Trust me though, everyone goes through those times of desperation and the parenting fails (we just hope there's no one with a camera around), as that's real life, not social media life!

Just for the record, I am not a doctor and cannot give medical advice. Anything written in my book is from my research and assumptions. Crystals, energy healing and all of Babyopathy should be used as complementary therapies and not as a replacement for your GP's advice or medical care.

My sensory toolkits include:

Aromatherapy *(smell)*

Sadly, many women fear the use of essential oils during pregnancy and in particular during the first trimester, yet will not think twice about putting a chemical-based product in their bath (bubble bath or bath bombs) or on their hands (soap or perfumes) or sprayed into the air (air-fresheners) – all of which are much more harmful than the correct use of essential oils and I am sure some are potentially extremely toxic. Oh, but most likely will also still have essential oils in too as they are the basis of most aromatic products.

Question: Did you use shampoo/body wash/hairspray today?

We use all of these products without questioning what is in them and any harm they could be doing but shy away from many natural products. So, let's investigate just what is safe to use in pregnancy – when you are working under the guidance of a trained aromatherapist, which I am.

IFPA, International Federation of Professional Aromatherapists, Pregnancy Guidelines states:

The placental barrier

Essential oils by their very nature, being organic substances, will cross the placental barrier and have the potential to affect the foetus. However, the amount of essential oil that actually accesses the mother's skin is very tiny and therefore the amount that reaches the placenta is miniscule if proper dilutions are being used. Small amounts of essential oils can be beneficial to the baby and there are no recorded instances of harm being caused to the child through essential oils used in aromatherapy massage or inhalation.

NB: Do not use on baby's skin or with epilepsy/heart disease/diabetes

Essential Oils Safe to Use During Pregnancy
Taken from *Essential Oil Safety* by Robert Tisserand & Rodney Young

Benzoin	Cypress	Juniper	Neroli
Bergamot	Eucalyptus	Lavender	Peppermint*
Black Pepper	Frankincense	Lemon	Pettigrain
Chamomile- (German)	Geranium	Mandarin	Rose Otto
	Ginger	Marjoram	Sandalwood
Chamomile – (Roman)	Grapefruit	Melissa*	Sweet Orange
			Tea Tree
Clary Sage*			

*Only to be used during labour as part of Babyopathy Birthing Programme and/or by a trained consultant

Essential oils bathe your entire body with their beautiful aromas that through your olfactory system (sense of smell) have a direct path to your brain and in turn can nurture your emotional and mental well-being. They can also nourish your skin and through direct absorption nurture your internal well-being too!

My complete range of Babyopathy Essential Oils for Pregnancy, Birth & Beyond are produced and sold by Base Formula, one of the UK's largest and most respected manufacturers of oils.

They can be purchased from their website:
www.baseformula.com

Music Therapy (sound)

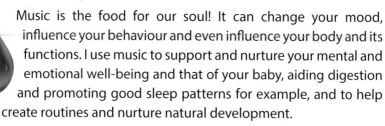

Music is the food for our soul! It can change your mood, influence your behaviour and even influence your body and its functions. I use music to support and nurture your mental and emotional well-being and that of your baby, aiding digestion and promoting good sleep patterns for example, and to help create routines and nurture natural development.

Sadly, the power and beauty of different music is being lost and you have to be a 'geek', old (or worse label) to listen to classical or jazz music for example. Yet they all have some amazing benefits to our mental and emotional well-being and even our physical well-being, and I for one am leading a music and singing revolution!

Meditation (sound)

Meditation is a miracle tool and I have included it under sound as many people use a guided meditation or music and chanting for example. When used properly it can bring peace and balance to your mind, help you to de-stress and relax and support learning, development and even your work life. Who doesn't want that?

Meditation does not need to be hours of chanting, although chanting does have its benefits and I do find it will get even the most stubborn child to sleep. You can use the techniques of breathing for example for a quick de-stress right through to a regular meditation session every day. Anything that means you can 'switch off' for a little every day, to feel the benefits of your body relaxing and your mind slowing will bring enormous benefits to you and your baby. My favourite is just walking by the river or in a forest or sitting by the sea and just immersing in the therapeutic sounds, colour and healing beauty of nature.

My complete range of pregnancy and birth meditations have been written specifically to help you through your entire journey of becoming a mum (there's even one for dads too!) with the music written by musician Chris Kimber. Meditation is key to being a relaxed mum and can also contribute to a positive pregnancy and birth experience, and even help with pain relief!

The meditations can be downloaded from here: www.store.cdbaby.com/cd/chriskimber10

Heka Balancing *(touch)*

Many people are aware of reiki as a 'healing' tool (which I am a Master/Teacher in). However, within Babyopathy and Nascuropathy we practise heka balancing as we believe people aren't 'broken' so don't need fixing; they are all unique, just like babies, and so just need support and some balance in their life. Heka balancing is part of all of my Babyopathy toolkits but is not mandatory by any means and certainly not for everyone, but I love it!

Putting it simply, heka balancing connects us to the energy of all life to bring balance wherever we may need it, using a variety of sensory tools such as crystals, music, aromatherapy etc. It brings relaxation and works to eliminate stress, and we all know the damaging effects stress can have on our mind, body and soul. It reconnects us where we have been disconnected and nourishes our own energy field with positive and nurturing energy.

I have been part of some amazing heka journeys with people, and like all my advice, start something new before you are pregnant so that you benefit the most from the experience, or wait until after the first trimester. As you progress through your trimesters, heka is an amazing way to build a connection with your baby.

I am often asked 'what should I think about?' during a heka session and there is no right or wrong answer, but I find that as it is your energy that is being supported, it makes sense for you to think about what you personally would like to achieve from the heka. So, whether that is to help you relax, or lose weight or have an easy birth, the choice is yours. It is just a starting point for your mind to think about until you naturally drift off into your own relaxation space.

To find out more you can visit my consultancy website: www.angelajspencer.co.uk

Crystals *(touch)*

I often get a weird look when I mention heka and then when I introduce crystals there can be raised eyebrows. However, crystals like every living thing have a vibrational energy that can nurture us in many ways supporting our sleep patterns, our mental and emotional well-being and much more.

It is very important that you take good advice from someone who has trained and qualified as a crystal practitioner, as like any complementary therapy, it shouldn't be played with and I have seen people charging phenomenal amounts without the knowledge to back up what they are doing. We can all read things on the internet and claim to be an expert but I have been taught by the wonderful Shirley O'Donoghue of Lucis College (also my Reiki Master/ Teacher) and she teaches crystals by intuition. You have to feel the vibrational energy of each crystal and the person you are working with to understand the crystals they need. You have to know their contraindications and beneficial properties. Yes, a few of these can be generalised and used accordingly as I show you in this book, but to be effective crystals have to be cleaned and have their intentions set and can also be empowered by heka energy. So, working with a professional is vital.

The power of crystals is widely recognised, Quartz has been used in watches and in particular very expensive watches for many years. Mums embrace their power by using Amber directly on a baby's skin to help with teething – even royalty, with the Duchess of Sussex said to be wearing crystals to help her through her pregnancy. In Babyopathy, I use them to help bathe your own energy with a veritable bubble bath of positive and balancing energy to nurture your emotional well-being, support some physical symptoms like nausea for example, to help mum and baby sleep and aid the birthing process. Personally, I wear crystals (whichever ones I feel I need) every day and still love seeing the difference from when someone walks into my consultation room to how they walk out after using crystals (and heka).

Nutrition *(taste)*

Many people underestimate the power of nutrition. We know how we feel if we overeat or eat something that doesn't agree with us and so it also goes that nutrition can make us feel better, happier and healthier. I work with a wonderful nutritionist by the name of Debbie Best whom I have known for many years and whose knowledge I trust implicitly.

We now blindly eat products from the supermarket but yet have no idea how they were produced or what they actually contain. Even some of our fruit and vegetables could contain harmful pesticides, be genetically modified or even have gained more air miles than the average person, and don't get me started about the meat and poultry trade.

I am often asked if I recommend 'going organic' and I know this can cause annoyance to some as organic can be more expensive. However, I don't think there is a need for everything to be organic in our diets. I personally will use organic milk and meat wherever possible and soft skin fruits for example, but I am also a great advocate for growing your own! My dad's cucumbers beat the supermarket variety hands down and before you shout that some don't have gardens etc., my dad grows much of his in vertical boxes now, due to his age and inability to garden the traditional way, which could even be done on a balcony. In truth, it is probably the time and effort that is needed that is more of the obstacle and excuse than the space (there are allotments or community projects too of course).

I will say this though, that if we really took notice of what we are eating and how it was produced we may feel so much healthier and need less medication. My daughter and I have insulin resistance due to our endometriosis, so we struggle to control our weight and what we eat; even just changing our milk and meat can have a huge effect on the symptoms we suffer.

Eating healthily (even with some organic thrown in) is not necessarily more expensive. If you plan and buy what you need rather than just buy as you walk around (this used to be my bad habit) you will be amazed at just how much more of the good stuff you can actually buy even including enough for my super sauces! Buying in bulk when on offer, cooking and freezing is also another great way to save money and know you have some ready-made meals or sauces etc. ready to go in the freezer too.

Colour Psychology *(sight)*

We all understand the power of colour psychology whether you realise it or not. For example, how different do you feel when there is a beautiful clear blue sky compared to a grey one? That is not just nature, it is the influence of colour and natural imagery and an important part of my Babyopathy toolkits. I was first introduced to the power of colour psychology back in 2000 by June McLeod when we first introduced it into my nurseries – what a transformation! The children were calmer, slept better and were happier – as noticed by very happy parents!

Chapter Two

The Pregnancy Journey and What You Should Know Before Travelling

babyopathy

Relaxed Mum, Contented Baby!

The Pregnancy Journey and What You Should Know Before Travelling

Very few people think about what they should do before having a baby nowadays and more and more we hear stories about women only finding out they are pregnant as they go into labour – now that is what you call a 'surprise'.

If you find yourself in this situation then this section will not help you in any way and there's no point stressing over the 'shoulda, woulda, coulda' (I'm sure there's an old song in those words!). In fact, if you've missed any of the stages then don't panic, it doesn't make you a bad parent, there is nothing here to be judged over and you can still be a relaxed mum! Just start at the stage you find yourself at and do what you can from there. There are no right or wrong choices (as long as they are not detrimental to you or your baby's health and well-being of course).

There is always something you can do from the point that you join Babyopathy to help you on your parenting journey so don't stress over what you 'missed' or didn't do. We all make choices that lead us to where we are and the only thing that we should worry about is the change that we can make today as that's the one that matters and the only one we can do anything about!

SO – YOU WANT TO HAVE A BABY?

Throughout my book I will tell you like it is. I am not saying anything to purposely offend anyone and am not looking for arguments, so don't bother trolling me (a sad side effect of the social media world we live in), but all of the things I cover in my book or say bluntly are things that mums I have worked with have said 'I wish someone had told me that.' So, although they might not be relevant to you (don't take offence just skip to the next bit), they will be relevant to someone and may help them.

First and foremost, you should want to have a baby for the right reasons, because I can categorically tell you:

A baby will not fix a broken relationship

If he already wants to leave, having a baby will not make him stay; even if he says he will stay he will not stay completely – he will at some stage blame you for 'making him stay' or eventually leave for the reasons he said he was leaving in the first place.

Having a baby is stressful and will put added stress on an already stressed relationship – it will not make things 'better'.

A baby is not a way to escape home

When you are young and feeling like you need to escape from what you feel are controlling parents or an unhappy childhood, having a baby and moving into a council-paid home is not the answer. More often than not you could be housed in a high-rise flat, isolated and alone at a time when you are young and vulnerable yourself. Instead, find someone you can trust and talk to who can help you find a way forward that is right for you and not a reason to escape.

A baby is not an accessory

Having a baby because you've seen all your celebrity idols doing it and getting paid to show off their bump, then baby in the latest fashions and 'must haves' with 100,000 followers on social media to boot is not real life! They won't and don't post about the bad days or the sleepless nights or the uncontrollable emotions and leakages. That isn't glamorous but that is real life and they all go through it but the social media craze just means you don't see it. The difference is they have people they can pay to help out, do their makeup and get them sponsorships – you don't. You will have to do it all the hard way!

So, having a baby for the **right reasons** is the first way to ensure you are a relaxed mum as you will not carry any emotional 'baggage' that whether you mean to or not, you (or your partner) can use or hold against your baby later on. Sadly, it happens.

Now you know you want to try for a baby, what should you do? The next way to be a relaxed mum is to **plan.**

Well, here is where I can give you, your first Babyopathy toolkit:

It's all about YOU!

The purpose behind this toolkit is probably one of the most important throughout your entire parenting journey as:

If you don't take care of yourself,
you can't take good care of your baby or family!
– Babyopathy Relaxed Mum motto!

So, you may as well start now…

Now it's important to understand there is no right or wrong time to have a baby. If you waited for all of the long list of 'perfect time' scenarios to fall into place you may as well say you will win the lottery tomorrow, the odds are probably the same. However, if you want a baby for the right reasons and now seems as good a time as any because you have an income, a home and a willing partner then here are some things you need to factor into your plan.

Nutrition

Did you know, what you eat in the months prior to falling pregnant can even determine the health of your baby's teeth. That's how important your diet is *before* you get pregnant.

Starting a healthy eating plan before you become pregnant is important for both your own health and well-being and that of your baby too. Gestational (pregnancy) diabetes is on the rise and I believe this is partly due to misinformation but also to the multitude of ready-made products that are convenient to our busy, stressful lives that contain much more sugar than we realise and other health-affecting ingredients than we need.

There are many quick and easy meals that can be made if you swap a shop-bought sauce for one of my super sauces, which can be made in bulk and frozen in portions (or add a super sauce into a basic passata for example) that will be much better for you and your future baby, adding maybe only 20 minutes to your busy schedule. Great to do throughout your pregnancy and for family life too, and no, I am not judging someone who feels like they do not have the time or feels like they can't afford it. In truth, if we want to do anything, we can, even in a small way or make a small change. It actually boils down to if we **want** to or not, and that is down to an individual's **choice**. I'm just giving you the tools, if you **want** to, not saying you have to.

However, you absolutely should also consider some additional supplements as our modern diets do not provide us with everything we need for everyday life let alone when pregnant.

Multi-vitamin with folic acid

Folic acid is an important supplement that should ideally be taken for at least three months before you fall pregnant. The synthetic form of vitamin B9, known as folic acid, helps prevent neural tube defects (NTDs) which are serious birth defects of the spinal cord such as spina bifida and the brain such as anencephaly. As these defects can occur in early stages of pregnancy (and sometimes before you may discover you are pregnant, which is why as much as possible we suggest you 'plan' to try for a baby), it is suggested that you start taking a good multi-vitamin containing folic acid at least three months before you start trying. I personally recommend the Pregnacare range from Vitabiotics.

Omega-3 fatty acids

Omega-3 fatty acids are an essential part of our diet that most of us do not consume enough of. However, research has shown that adequate consumption of omega-3 fatty acids during pregnancy is vital as they are critical building blocks of the foetal brain; they have also shown potential in the prevention of post-natal depression. Again, Vitabiotics produce a pregnancy vitamin and omega-3 formula combined.

Nutritional supplement

Even following a healthy eating plan, it is very difficult to eat the now recommended '10 a day'. In order to boost the vitamins and minerals your body will need on this journey, and it is a journey, I also recommend taking Juice Plus (the chewables as they do not contain additional folic acid); this is just a personal recommendation and not a medical one. They can be expensive and so is not a 'must have' unlike the folic acid and omega-3.

Whilst talking about nutrition, I have been contacted a lot (and seen many forums) about losing weight/dieting while pregnant. I have to say, wherever possible, if you think you need to lose weight then *plan* to do so before you get pregnant. Get healthy for the journey ahead as once you are on that 'train' you do not want to be restricting yourself when it comes to what you or your baby need. Even if it means waiting a few extra months to start trying, get to that healthy weight or turn around your eating habits now as dieting can affect your energy, your hormones, your mood and more and you will have enough of that going on just being pregnant!

Now, one of the other things I want to talk about has no proven links and technically is a theory of mine but it is advice I am giving to my own daughter when she wants to try for a baby so I'm putting it out there for you to use, or not, it is completely down to you.

Let's talk about water. It is something that you need lots of and with sliced lemon in will become your friend in the first trimester. However, I was asked to look at reasons for the increase in infertility for an article and I found some worrying potential issues.

When it comes to water, we expect the water that comes from our taps to be high-quality water and beneficial to our health, right? Well, it seems that may not always be the case (and if you are reading this in the USA I found some awful information about water supplies so please look into it). Water treatment plants should remove pretty much most things during its processes; however, one of the things it cannot remove completely is contraceptive drugs. Now, in all the 'official' documents I could find it says that the levels of contraceptives found in drinking water are negligible and therefore *should* not have any adverse effects. However, I have to wonder if this is maybe a contributing factor to rising infertility as contraceptives have been circulating in increasing amounts over the last 40 or so years. I am not scaremongering but my advice to my daughter is to drink good quality bottled water from a company that does not use BPA* in their bottles.

*Bisphenol A, BPA, is found in polycarbonate plastics and epoxy resins. Polycarbonate plastics are often used in containers that store food and beverages, such as water bottles. BPA is a concern because of possible health effects of BPA on the brain, behaviour and prostate gland of foetuses, infants and children.

Get your body ready

If there is one thing I wish someone had told me before I got pregnant it's just how much toll a pregnancy can take on your body! My energy levels were zapped and my body stretched beyond normal human proportions (I think I must have the 'Mrs Incredible' stretchy gene – although my stomach never went back to the svelte figure she had but my bottom stayed as big as hers!).

Yoga is one of the best ways to prepare your body for its own personal journey ahead; things will need to stretch, things will need to be squashed and your bladder control will be tested to the max. It is also something that you can continue with throughout your pregnancy.

. . . .

TOP TIP: *If your body is used to exercise before you get pregnant then you can carry on, with good, authoritative advice throughout.*

. . . .

If you want to lose weight, then again, now before you fall pregnant is the time to do it and starting an exercise regime you can continue throughout your pregnancy is the best way.

If you are not into yoga or don't want to pay for lessons or a gym membership then good old-fashioned walking is brilliant. In fact, even if you do join a gym or have yoga lessons, get out and walk too. Walking in nature (by a river, in a park or forest or just the nearest bit of greenery you can find) has been proven to support your emotional and mental well-being as well as your fitness level. So, you tick the Babyopathy box and it's free to do! Feeling fit and being out and about contributes hugely to being relaxed and being positive.

If there is one by-product of this book and Babyopathy in general we hope to achieve, it's positivity! As the entire pregnancy journey, including fertility and conception, seems to have become hugely negative, a struggle, and in many cases expensive and a source of disappointment and misery. It doesn't have to be and shouldn't be that way – and being a 'relaxed mum' is the key to returning to the positive side!

Whilst we are talking bodies, I think we should mention EMF waves (electromagnetic fields) and the potential effect they can have on fertility, and it is not just a concern for women but men too. Through my research I have come across a multitude of studies that have looked at the effects of EMF on our health and well-being. The conclusions drawn from these studies have cited risks such as affecting infertility/miscarriage/childhood cancer and genetic/developmental disruptions.

We have all read the news articles claiming brain tumours have been caused by mobile phone use; however it is not just about holding a phone to our ears to talk. Many of us carry our phone in our pockets and for men this is right next to some very important 'tackle'. Studies have shown that men who are exposed to levels of magnetic fields of only 0.16 microtesla (μT) for six or more hours a day were four times as likely to have substandard sperm.

I used to carry my mobile in my jeans pocket, always the right one as I am right handed – is it a coincidence I developed a tumour on my right ovary? Thankfully it was benign, but I lost my ovary to it. So, although no official statements are made regarding EMFs from mobile phones, wifi networks or power lines, again is it coincidence that there is a huge rise in couples (both men and women) needing help to conceive?

Personally, I do think there is a potential effect of EMF on fertility, and a study by Bellieni (2012) found that the induced current in a laptop's power supply exceeded ICNIRP levels in adults and the unborn babies of pregnant mothers. So, if it can do that, it makes sense to keep the laptop away from your lap. Better safe than sorry!

Your mental well-being

Very few people, me included when I was younger, think about their own mental health well-being until it's too late and we are in the depths of depression or worse. Despite all of the media surrounding mental health it still seems to be a taboo and I want to change that.

Our **Before Travelling Workshop** was created to give all potential mums a chance to talk about the pregnancy 'journey' and the 'whys' and the 'what on earths' they will encounter along the way but it also allows us to introduce our Mentor Mums programme. Mentor Mums is all about having someone you can trust to support you on this lifelong journey and talk about anything with. Find out more in the Mentor Mums section.

The workshop also includes an introduction to our meditations which helps you to control your stress levels throughout your pregnancy and there is a very good reason for doing so. Our Routine in the Womb campaign highlights the effects of stress on the unborn baby, and these effects can have influence throughout the whole of your pregnancy. Dr Calvin Hobel, a perinatologist in Los Angeles in an interview with WebMD.com stated:

> *"Stress is a silent disease," says Dr Hobel, director of maternal-foetal medicine at Cedars Sinai and a professor of obstetrics/gynaecology and paediatrics at University of California, Los Angeles (UCLA). "Pregnant women need to be educated in recognizing when they have stress, the consequences and some of the simple things they can do to make a difference."*

Dr Pathik Wadhwa, assistant professor of behavioural science, obstetrics and gynaecology at University of Kentucky College of Medicine continued with:

> *"Pre-term births and low birth weight are among the most recognized effects of maternal stress during pregnancy, established over nearly two decades of animal and human research."*

Recent studies by Dr Wadhwa and colleagues suggest that women who experience high levels of psychological stress are significantly more likely to deliver pre-term. Typically, one in 10 women delivers pre-term (before 37 weeks).

> *"Pre-term babies are susceptible to a range of complications later, including chronic lung disease, developmental delays, learning disorders and infant mortality. There's even compelling evidence from epidemiological studies and animal research that babies who experience stress in utero (in the*

womb) are more likely to develop chronic health problems as adults, such as heart disease, high blood pressure and diabetes.

Another stress response is more likely to affect foetal growth and pre-term labour. That is, when pregnant women experience stress, particularly in the first trimester, the placenta increases production of corticotropin-releasing hormone (CRH), which regulates the duration of pregnancy and foetal maturation.

CRH is one of the most exciting recent scientific discoveries that could explain why women go into labour when they do. Called the 'placental clock,' CRH levels measured in the mother's blood early in pregnancy -- between 16 and 20 weeks -- can predict the onset of labour months later. Those with the highest levels will likely deliver prematurely, and those with lowest levels are apt to deliver past their due dates."

I have included these statements as they are fact and from experts conducting constant research and it is not to scare you in any way but to highlight the importance of learning ways to de-stress or manage your stress better from the very beginning. It is much better to hear these facts **before** you find out you are pregnant as they are less scary then and hopefully just make you determined to find a de-stress routine right from the start. That way, anything that happens or you come across when you are pregnant is already in hand – you got this!

In theory, meditation can also help you to fall pregnant. OK, so there is nothing to prove that meditation can help with your fertility or to fall pregnant, **but**… there is proof that meditation can help to reduce your stress and anxiety levels, that it can be beneficial to your mental and emotional well-being, and help your body to regulate itself because of the reduction in stress hormones such as cortisol and all of those things that affect your fertility and ability to fall pregnant – so I rest my case.

Being aware of your own mental health well-being, what makes you stressed and building a relationship with someone you trust that you can talk to about it is vital in your quest to be a relaxed mum for your baby. You are the key to their well-being, so taking care of you, being able to openly talk about things that are worrying you without being judged or made to feel like a failure is one of the most important things you can do for your baby – and you!

Heka Balancing

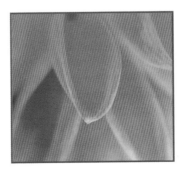

I would thoroughly recommend finding a heka practitioner you are comfortable working with before you are pregnant. As with everything, if you are going to start something new, start it before you fall pregnant. Our heka practitioners have to spend many hours not only learning but also treating others and providing case studies.

Heka is a wonderful way to become tuned into your body and eventually your baby. It is also a great tool to use to de-stress and relax, which is vital when it comes to conceiving.

I ask my 'Babyopathy Mummas' to focus on what they want to achieve from their heka balancing while they first start to relax for a treatment; I say this but almost without fail everyone has either fallen asleep or relaxed so deeply they have long forgotten to 'think'. So, for example, when you are wanting to conceive I suggest thinking about your body relaxing and everything finding a balance whilst sending beautiful 'healing pink rays' to your entire reproductive system – and then let heka do the rest as you drift away…

It's All About You - Babyopathy Toolkit

Smell - Oils

Grapefruit Is a wonderful zesty oil that when inhaled will help to curb your cravings when trying to lose weight.

Use as an inhaler to curb food cravings and stick to regular mealtimes.

It's All About You
This beautiful blend has been created to help you as you begin your meditation and relaxation journey (and can be used by you before pregnancy and help you take care of you!
Do not use if you think you may be pregnant.

Use in a diffuser during your meditation sessions to help you achieve your goals or can be added to a bath or massage oil.

Touch - Crystals

Moonstone is the ultimate feminine stone and believed to be the talisman of lovers so I can't think of a better stone to help you on your journey and ensure a beautiful bond between you.

Moonstone – wear from pre-pregnancy but don't forget to take off and re-charge on the windowsill during a full moon!

Chrysophrase is part of the chalcedony family which is nurturing for pregnancy and newborns. It opens, activates and energises both the heart and sacral chakras and as such balances and supports your reproductive system and so fertility.

When you are ready to start trying for a baby we add in Chrysophrase to wear and use during heka.

	Babyopathy 'Fertility' Bracelet	
Touch - Crystals (Cont'd)	I created this beautiful bracelet to balance, nurture and support the reproductive system, your emotional well-being and of course, spread the love in your relationship!	**Wear throughout the day and place by your bed at night** (don't wear during the full moon as it includes Moonstone).
 **Heka Balancing**	I always tell my clients to focus on what they want to achieve from my treatments. At this stage, you can focus on your own specific goals that will help you get to that all important conception!	I would recommend having your first heka session and keeping a diary for a week, and then have another, you can then give good feedback to your practitioner. I personally would recommend having heka balancing at least once a month but I see my Babyopathy Mums up to once a week.
Sound - Meditation	It's All About You Any meditation you can do will help you to relax and de-stress but this meditation has been written specifically to help you achieve your pre-pregnancy goals!	Meditation in the morning is a great way to start the day and give you some extra energy and focus.

The Relaxed Mum CHECKLIST

✓ **You want a baby for the right reasons**

✓ **You have time to plan and get ready for a pregnancy**

✓ **You have your Mentor Mum at the ready**

✓ **You have your Babyopathy Toolkit and a de-stress routine**

A little disclaimer – if you are unable to do the above, if you choose not to do any of the above or you simply missed out on doing any of the above, it does not make you a bad parent or exclude you from being a relaxed mum; I am simply bringing you all of the information (or as much as possible) together in one place, to help you make informed choices for both your own well-being and that of your baby – the choice remains yours.

Chapter Three

Mentor Mums and
Why You Need One

Relaxed Mum, Contented Baby!

Mentor Mums and Why You Need One

I have included Mentor Mums at this stage because I think now more than ever is when they are needed. It is good to have someone you trust to talk to throughout your entire pregnancy, someone who can come to appointments if need be, or just at the end of a phone, but in the first weeks and beyond they are vital.

For many it will be their mum, but sadly not everyone has their mum with them or close by, or maybe they just don't have that relationship with them. So, I created the Mentor Mum movement which is growing with every consultant that comes on board. I have been a Mentor Mum to many and duties have ranged from the odd conversation by text through to attending every appointment and being called 'surrogate mum'. It is a role I relish as however small my contribution, I know 'every little helps' – I hope that's not a licensed catch phrase!

If you can, choose who your Mentor Mum will be right from the start. They need to know the role they are signing up for as any question goes, no subject is off limits or taboo! You need to be able to ask anything and, trust me, I have been! It usually starts with 'I'm so embarrassed to ask' or 'I don't know how to put it' but if a question is there then you need an answer, so you should never be worried about asking it.

They also need to be experienced enough to see the signs you might not, to notice if you need something and support you through the journey no matter what. However, this kind of works both ways, you have to respect who they are too, and if they have a concern they should be able to voice it with you without worrying about your reaction.

There is more info on our Mentor Mum Programme on our website.

Babyopathy Classes - Classes for Mums – Run by Mums

I decided to launch Babyopathy classes for parents as I was so disheartened listening to so much bad advice and also seeing so many parents in need of support and someone to listen.

The day I sat down to originally start writing this book I read a very tragic story of a 39-year-old new mother who took her own life just 10 weeks after giving birth as she was suffering from post-natal depression. This new mum, like me, had terrible trouble feeding her new daughter. The infuriating current obsession with 'breast is best' led her to feel she was incompetent and a bad mother simply because she could not produce enough milk for her baby and the post-natal depression exacerbated these feelings. Yes, she had a loving husband who did all he could to help his wife whilst also trying to care for their baby. Yes, they both had a loving family who did all they could to help with the rest of everyday life, but what they didn't have was someone who listened.

My heart goes out to this family and others who find themselves in circumstances beyond their control.

My aim with Babyopathy is to give new mums the reassurance that they **are** doing great, but as we have already established, there is no such thing as:

- ✿ *A perfect pregnancy*
- ✿ *A perfect birth*
- ✿ *A perfect baby (OK I know I say every baby is perfect, but you know what I mean here)*
- ✿ *A perfect mum*

Every baby, every family, every mum and the life they lead is unique and all we can do is always try our best, and if at first we don't succeed, try something else!

If you're struggling to breastfeed and are at your wits end, try a bottle, it won't mean they will never breastfeed again but it will mean they are fed and you can try again when they are not so frustrated. If your baby won't sleep at night, sleep with them during the day until you can encourage a different routine. If you feel like you aren't coping, talk to another mum who will tell you, 'you're doing great, just like the rest of us, but there's always help if you need it'. It is important to realise that you're not alone and you ask for help.

Our hour-long classes give parents an insight into some of the activities they can do at home with very little cost. The activities are based around treasure baskets linked to different areas of the home, so it encourages parents to interact with their babies using things that can be found around the house and not expensive toys.

Our class consultants act as Mentor Mums and each week we have a Hot Topic sheet that gives a basis for a discussion that sometimes spins off into all kinds of directions with issues that the group of mums (and dads sometimes too) feel they need to talk about. In addition, we provide parents with an activity sheet based around the developmental benefits and how parents can continue to encourage their baby's development at home.

Our classes help you and your baby to:

- ✿ *Experience... baby-led development through interactive, sensory-based activities using natural resources and support for mum*
- ✿ *Explore and encourage... age appropriate development*
- ✿ *Record... your child's experiences and achievement*

We have had an overwhelming response from parents about our classes and friendships have formed that we hope last a lifetime.

Chapter Four
The Thin Blue Line Appears - First Trimester

babyopathy

Relaxed Mum, Contented Baby!

The Thin Blue Line Appears
- First Trimester

Back to your pregnancy journey! The thin blue line has appeared in both windows – congratulations! The starting line of your pregnancy journey has been drawn, now where?

I am sure you want to tell the world but the big debate now seems to be just when should you share the news with everyone? As with everything in this book it is about what will help you be a relaxed mum, so when is the right time for you? Take a moment to think about everything below and then be happy with the decision you make, that's all that matters!

Years ago you could almost be through your first trimester before your pregnancy could be confirmed as even morning sickness may just be a stomach bug and tests weren't that effective. Now, not only can you complete a test a week before your period is due, you can even complete a test that tells you if you are ovulating – what a leap in technology.

The problem with this though is whether a pregnancy is viable, because years ago if it wasn't, you most likely would miscarry and put it down to your period 'just being late' without the upset of knowing it was actually an early miscarriage. The other side of this is that we did not dwell on the fact it may have been an early miscarriage; our period was just late for some reason and we let it go from a mental well-being point of view.

Now we know; we know if we have an early miscarriage because we know if we are pregnant almost immediately, and it is contributing to our stress, and in many cases contributing to the added stresses of trying for a baby, and most definitely contributing to fertility worries many seem to have. Sadly, not every conception will produce a viable pregnancy and nature will take its course. I have been there myself, I can tell you what the doctor said to me when I had a miscarriage at eight weeks, 'Our bodies are made to have babies and if it is a viable pregnancy it will make it through, and if it is not, nature will do its job and you have to trust nature.'

It sounds like a very harsh statement and I apologise if you think that makes me sound harsh too, but for me it made sense and helped me deal with the miscarriage and be positive to try again. If I had dwelled on the miscarriage and worried over it I would have caused myself added stress and lessened my chances of falling pregnant again and with a viable pregnancy. Yes, I talked about it and yes, I cried, and if that's what you need to do you absolutely should. Never hold in grief because you are worried what someone else may think. But I also knew we wanted a baby and so my focus went to what I could do, be healthy and be positive for the next pregnancy.

Why am I saying all of this? Well our mental health well-being is at its all-time low or most fragile, however you want to look at it, and our mental health well-being can have an effect on our fertility and our ability to carry a baby to full term. We are affected by stress now more than ever, and worse than that is the effect social media is having on our lives. It has given a platform for faceless bullies, body and people shaming, trolling and the list goes on.

It is having a disastrous effect on our mental health well-being and I believe also our relationships and future lives, and I want to share the message that it needs to stop. We need to start a new trend of mums supporting mums, of no judgment and of positivity.

I can't change when you find out you're pregnant because that's life now. However, what I can do is give you as many tools as possible to help you through not just this trimester but all three as happy and healthy as I can.

So, when should you tell everyone you're pregnant? Well that is completely down to you. If you want to tell everyone as soon as you find out then do, and if you would rather wait until your first scan then that is what's right for you. The risk of miscarriage drops to 0.5% by week nine and so the old-fashioned 'must wait until 12 weeks and first scan' is kind of irrelevant. I think the reason most people wait until their scan is because it doesn't 'feel' real; if you have no other symptoms (and not everyone does) the scan at least proves there's a baby in there!

I quite like the new trends of pregnancy announcements, there's some really cute ideas out there. My daughter just handed me the positive pregnancy test, but then I had been helping them on their pre-pregnancy journey anyway. She then waited until their first early scan (it was at nine weeks due to her risks from endometriosis) and gave close family an announcement box but waited until after the 20 weeks scan to tell everyone else and put it on social media – with some very cute Disney announcement pictures.

Overall it should be something you can share positively and without worrying about what anyone will say, or what will happen – it's your moment so choose it and enjoy it!

One piece of advice I would give is to tell your employers (not all your co-workers necessarily), in writing, of your early stage of pregnancy, as managing stress at work is just as important in this trimester. More in the Routine in the Womb section.

The sensory journey begins!

Now you're pregnant, but just when exactly does your baby's sensory journey begin? Well, all of your baby's senses begin to develop around eight weeks after conception but are not functioning yet, you'll have to wait until the second trimester for that and 24 weeks for your baby to actually have a conscious sensory connection. More on that later.

Your sensory journey during the first trimester is something else though.

At the beginning, there is you! OK, if you want to get technical, dad is there too (or at least a contribution from him is, medical science can be a wonderful thing!) but after that fleeting second of conception, it's all you.

You carry the baby in your womb, you have a maternal bond before you even realise it, and from the very start I encourage you to use Babyopathy to interact with your baby and continue to be a relaxed mum.

One of the first realisations that you may be pregnant is morning sickness and boy what fun that can be! However, there are a few sensory tricks that you can try to alleviate it:

> **Ginger** – *a miracle food when it comes to morning sickness, my favourite was to eat a ginger biscuit before I even got out of bed (and if you can persuade someone to bring you a cup of tea with it even better!). However, they are full of sugar (and only a small amount of ginger) so if you can eat ginger other ways it is better.*

> **Peppermint** – *is brilliant whether as an essential oil to sniff if you are feeling nauseous or as a tea to sip (during the first trimester is fine but it can decrease milk production so avoid from third trimester onwards), it is great for settling your stomach too. Not for use in direct skin treatments though.*

> **Lemon** – *is a great friend of the pregnant woman; if you are feeling faint, inhaling lemon oil on a tissue can help revive you and slices of lemon in some water will keep you hydrated and can help with nausea.*

> **Yellow Jade** – *I fully believe that we are all of our senses combined and therefore if you combine the power of the lemon oil, you can put drops on a lava bracelet, which has been made with Yellow Jade stones which support your solar plexus chakra and digestive system, you have a double-barrelled morning sickness attack system! Yellow Jade also supports pregnancy and dispels negativity, perfect!*

Throughout your pregnancy your senses will come alive, some women say their sense of smell becomes heightened, for others it's taste. Some things that you always tolerated will now become your worst nightmare, others will become an absolute craving. It is quite normal so don't worry although I would suggest eating wall plaster or coal (yes, I saw that Discovery Channel programme too!) is not to be recommended.

Your sensory journey whilst pregnant can have both a positive and negative effect on you and your baby. You may think that your baby is tucked away nice and cosy, but they can be affected too as I have already talked about.

One of the biggest things that can have an effect on your baby during your pregnancy is stress and this can have an impact from as early as six weeks of pregnancy. Stress can be caused in many ways and sometimes it is unavoidable especially if you have a demanding job. There is more on this in the Routine in the Womb Hero chapter.

Over the three trimesters I will give you different ways that you can use Babyopathy throughout your pregnancy to help you relax and deal with the stresses that your job or running around after your older children may bring and help create a routine that you can carry on when the baby is born.

Touch

Suggested crystal – MOONSTONE
Ultimate stone for pregnancy and birth – encourages calm!

(crystals should be placed in a room where activity is predominantly taking place or worn as a piece of jewellery)

However, whilst talking about stress, I want to talk for a moment about personal situations and I know this can be a sensitive subject so am just going to say it and get it out there.

If you are in a situation or a relationship where you find yourself in constant arguments or even a violent encounter then this will have an effect on your baby because of the hormones your body releases during these stressful situations. It is not positive for anyone's well-being to be in these situations and I urge you to talk to someone you feel you can trust to help you find a solution.

Sadly, as I am writing, a TV celebrity/actress announced she has suffered a stress-induced miscarriage due to her very public and very volatile relationship. This not only highlights the risk of stress to unborn babies but also reiterates why social media and announcing every aspect of our lives is not always such a good thing.

Getting help is never something to be ashamed of or you should be made to feel guilty about. Asking for help in dealing with a difficult situation is something you should be proud of yourself for, because you are not only looking after your own well-being but putting the needs of your baby first – that is what Super Heroes do!

Nutrition

Now I know if you are suffering with morning sickness, food is probably the last thing on your mind. However, just like before pregnancy, your nutrition during your pregnancy is vitally important to the health and well-being of your baby.

The old wives' tale of 'eating for two' is just that as far as quantity is concerned. However, the quality of your diet for both of you is key.

Poor nutrition during pregnancy can have an impact on the growth and development of your baby in the womb, which can in turn have an effect on their future health and development –
Dr David Barker hypothesises:

Coronary heart disease/type 2 diabetes/stroke and hypertension originate in developmental plasticity in response to under nutrition during foetal life.

Dr David Barker's (MD, PHD, FRCP) paper 'Maternal Nutrition, Foetal Nutrition, and Disease in Later Life' from the MRC Environmental Epidemiology Unit, University of Southampton, Southampton General Hospital, Southampton, UK first popularised the concept of foetal origins of adult disease (FOAD). Since its inception, FOAD has received considerable attention. The FOAD hypothesis holds that events during early development have a profound impact on one's risk for development of future adult disease. Low birth weight, a surrogate marker of poor foetal growth and nutrition, is linked to coronary artery disease, hypertension, obesity, and insulin resistance.

Copyright © 2011 Mosby, Inc.

Please don't panic though, this is just information to help you make the right decisions for both your health and that of your baby. To help you I have put together the N-Plan, my healthy eating plan that encourages you to eat five fruits **and** five vegetables, one each from the five food colour groups every day – it's a challenge but oh so good for you! If you are pregnant, follow the full plan so that you are eating the correct amount of calories. If you are dieting before pregnancy, then cut out the treats and ensure you are exercising.

NB: The N-Plan A5 sheets can be downloaded when you register through my website.

So to re-cap:

- ✿ *Eat regularly and don't skip meals – even with morning sickness just try to eat little and often until it passes*
- ✿ *You don't need to eat for two, just eat healthily – an extra 200 calories a day during the last trimester is all that's needed (I will remind you!)*
- ✿ *If you are struggling to eat fruit and vegetables you can always make up some of the Super Sauces in The First Year chapter and include them in your meals*

Just as important as what you eat is what you drink. It is very important, if you know you are pregnant, to avoid alcohol and too much caffeine (cola as well as coffee) as it increases the risks of health concerns to your baby. There is so much evidence on this I don't think I need to include it here.

However, I would like to remind you to drink water. You should increase the amount of water you drink each day when pregnant, we don't drink enough as it is, but it will help you to combat nausea (again, especially with some cut-up lemon in it) and it will reduce the risk of fainting and of course, dehydration. This is most important if you are travelling/commuting or working – I apologise for the side effect of increased loo visits though, that's a natural body issue beyond my control. Blood flow to your kidneys increases anywhere between 30-60% and combine that with pregnancy hormones and additional bodily fluids means frequent toilet visits. Knowing where every accessible public toilet is will be your friend on your pregnancy journey!

Meditation/Music

Meditation/mindfulness, call it what you wish but it is your friend throughout your pregnancy. Yes, I know women have been having babies for millennia but in the last few decades our lives have changed drastically. This is why I developed the campaign Routine in the Womb which you can read later and you will have already read about the effect of stress throughout pregnancy in the Before Travelling section. It is most important now with the steps you take throughout your entire pregnancy to commit to the health of your pregnancy and in particular to have a positive pregnancy, in every way, including positive mental health – it is **not** a taboo!

We are surrounded by negativity nowadays. Social media should be an amazing way to connect with long-lost friends or distant relatives but sadly it has become a tool for bullying and trolling – I have had first-hand experience of it. Mental health concerns are increasing at an alarming rate and in particular maternal mental health, post-natal depression in dads and even mental health concerns in children from birth. I want to prevent this, to stop this trend, and I believe with Babyopathy and the toolkits I can certainly make a difference and it is the primary aim of this book – Relaxed Mum, Contented Baby!

This is why meditation is your friend as stress is a huge factor in supporting your mental health well-being. Stress is part of our modern lives and why I developed the **Thin Blue Line Workshop** to guide you through this first stage, when amazing things are happening in your belly – when the embryo becomes a foetus and the marvellous moment the baby's brain stem connects to their tiny developing brain.

The First Trimester Meditation is a great way to start your day especially when supported with the rest of the toolkit.

The Thin Blue Line - First Trimester Babyopathy Toolkit

Oils

Babyopathy First Trimester – Thin Blue Line Blend This gorgeous essential oil blend will help you to nurture those first connections for both you and your baby throughout this first trimester.	A beautiful blend for you to start your pregnancy meditation journey.
Lemon & Ginger Inhaler* not shown	Use as an inhaler with 2 drops of lemon and 3 drops of ginger to help with nausea.
Lavender * not shown Lavender is my 'all healer' when it comes to an essential oil. It relieves pain, de-stresses, helps you sleep and much more.	Headaches can be a common side effect of changing hormones or reactions to smells, lavender can be placed on to a wheat bag and placed across the eyes to help or a drop rubbed into your temples.

Rose Quartz

Rose Quartz is the love stone and it oozes harmony, balance and calm and of course, love. It is also known as the family stone which is perfect as you start the journey from a couple to a family.

Now you are pregnant Rose Quartz placed beside your bed is perfect for nurturing love and first bonds and your new journey. My Rose Quartz hearts can also be placed in the bath for five minutes before you get in so you literally bathe in its beauty!

Moonstone

We continue with Moonstone throughout pregnancy for its complete feminine protective properties

Crystals

Lemon or Yellow Jade

This is a gorgeous pale yellow stone used as a digestive aid and anti-emetic. Its nurturing properties also support long journeys, which you are now embarking on. It is also beneficial for building loving relationships, ideal for the new life growing inside you!

My gorgeous first trimester bracelet combines the power of Lemon Jade and Carnelian to support you through the first fears and symptoms of the first trimester, boosted by Snowflake Quartz and of course, Moonstone!

Crystals
(Cont'd)

Carnelian

Carnelian is a beautiful orange stone linked to the sacral chakra and therefore the reproductive system and supports and nurtures. However, if you have any particular fears and worries finding out you're pregnant (a previous miscarriage for example) then Carnelian helps to allay those worries.

As with any of the crystals, Carnelian can be placed beside your bed for you to soak up their vibrations as you sleep or by wearing them to be nurtured throughout the day.

Meditation

The Thin Blue Line – First Trimester

This wonderful meditation is all about those all-important first connections. It is a visualisation of your first connections with your baby and surrounding them with beautiful rays of energy to support the first connection of their brain stem that will light the spark of their senses.

Any meditation you can do will help you to relax and de-stress but this meditation has been written specifically to help you focus on the start of this amazing journey and those all-important first connections.

Heka Balancing

Health & Well-being

Heka during this trimester will surround your baby with nourishing, positive energy to support those all-important first connections and help you to relax and ensure you are stress free.

I always tell my clients to focus on what they want to achieve from my treatments. At this stage, you can focus on health and harmony, just what your baby needs!

The Relaxed Mum CHECKLIST

✓ Make the right choices for you as to when you tell everyone you are pregnant – and commit to 'mums supporting mums' – mental health matters

✓ Drink plenty of water (and always know where the nearest toilet is – trust me on this one!)

✓ You are 'eating for two' only from a well-being point of view (not in quantity)

✓ Meet your mental health well-being head on from day one – it is not a taboo

✓ You have your First Trimester Babyopathy Toolkit and are bathing in the beauty that is Rose Quartz

Chapter Five

Bump Day, Time to Bloom
- Second Trimester

babyopathy

Relaxed Mum, Contented Baby!

Bump Day, Time to Bloom
- Second Trimester

As 'hump' day is the new name for Wednesday, the middle of the week, we thought we would put our own spin on the middle of your pregnancy journey with 'bump day' and traditionally this middle three months is when mums start to bloom…

By the time you enter your second trimester you should hopefully have had your first midwife appointment and that all-important and absolutely amazing first scan! Almost a third of your pregnancy will have gone before you see a midwife and your baby for the first time.

It is an emotional moment beyond words when you first see that image on the black and white screen. The beating heart, the movements and the picture that for many will be the source of their baby's nickname! My first scan picture looked like a little alien but that name wasn't appropriate and out of nowhere her dad named her 'Wilf', I don't actually know what was worse! I was with my daughter for her first scan and she immediately said, 'It's a jellybean!' so that's how my granddaughter was known until she arrived.

Choosing a nickname is actually one of the first ways to begin bonding with your baby, for dad too as they struggle to bond at this stage because the only way the baby is really affecting them is through you, and most likely they are your outlet for vocalising your pregnancy niggles, your worries and stresses or just your demands for cravings! So, it's good to have a little fun and let them participate in a positive side of your pregnancy.

This is also the trimester your baby's senses come alive.

From the time your baby's brain stem connects at around 13 weeks in the womb, the beginning of the second trimester, your baby's senses will start to come alive and over the coming weeks they can:

💧 *HEAR*   *sounds, voice tones and music*

💧 *SEE*   *colour permeating through the womb*

💧 *SMELL* *through the amniotic fluid*

💧 *TASTE*   *what you have eaten through the amniotic fluid*

💧 *TOUCH* *you will at some stage feel the elbow under your ribs!*

In addition, they can also feel the emotions you feel, and this forms the basis for their natural instincts that they will use from the moment they are born (but they can also have an effect on their well-being – again, see the Routine in the Womb section). From that first moment, and after they are born, your baby will use their senses to be comforted and reassured through the sound of your voice and your smell, to feel secure by your touch and, of course, to let you know when they are hungry or tired! Throughout the book you will find colour-coded references for sensory stimulation to aid development or to support you and your baby's general well-being. Here's a brief introduction.

Sound   Sight   Smell   Taste   Touch

I am not going to tell you week by week what to expect in your pregnancy as there are so many books, websites and apps on that already, neither is this a 'must do' manual on bringing up your baby, it is sharing my knowledge, supporting you on your 'baby journey' and hopefully giving you the right information to make the right choices for you and your family.

Senses begin in the womb

For many mums that I've spoken to their pregnancy doesn't become 'real' to them until they feel the baby move, which is on average anywhere between 17 and 22 weeks (sometimes later or even earlier in subsequent pregnancies); again it is a sensory response that reinforces what we know to be true.

It is around this time also that all of your baby's sensory systems really start to develop, although first responses may have occurred earlier. From four to five months pre-natal your baby can, amongst other things:

- Hear for the first time, which is the inside of your body, which is why nature sounds such as whales (a bit like our bodies sound like from inside) or a washing machine (like our digestive system) can be soothing to a baby after birth
- *React to sound and will love rhythmic music*
  By third trimester can recognise rhythm and tones and mum's voice!
- *Loud sounds can make them jump!*
- You can use sound during third trimester to influence routine

- Baby's eyelids are closed until about 26 weeks
- *See light changes through the womb*
- By 32 weeks baby can track light i.e. a torch moved across the belly
- *By 33 weeks pupils dilate so they can see dim shapes*

- Suck their thumb
- *React to you massaging your belly (or the midwife having a prod to wake them!)*
- Explore their world in the womb
- *Touch is the strongest sense at birth*

- Around 13 weeks their sense of smell develops and they can actually smell aromas through the amniotic fluid
- *Babies can actually recognise their mother's smell at birth!*

- Taste develops between 13-15 weeks and happens via the amniotic fluid
- *By 21 weeks they can actually discern different flavours*
- Fussy eating habits can develop in the womb

NB: Anything with a purple petal is a **Babyopathy Top Tip** or a **whole sensory experience**

The emphasis for pregnant mums is quite often on nutrition and other health-related issues such as smoking, drinking and taking folate, and whilst this is important, just as crucial is the sensory world your 'bump' is exposed to.

For example, if you are having an argument, not only will your baby be able to hear the aggressive nature of those sounds but they will also 'feel' the effects of the stress hormones your body will be releasing. So, it is important to be aware of the negative influences and how we can nurture the positive ones.

I loved this stage of pregnancy and my **Bump Day Workshop** is one of my favourites as it is when you can really connect with your baby.

You can use your Second Trimester Toolkit to make those connections and sound is one of the senses you can have the most fun with:

- *Play your favourite music and have a boogie with your baby, feeling their movements (they will eventually recognise the tones and patterns in the music)*

- *You can enjoy a relaxing warm bath with some Babyopathy aromatherapy bath salts and massage your belly with our nourishing massage oil (great for your skin as it starts to stretch) and your baby will relax too and may even begin to respond to your touch*

- *Use meditation and heka balancing to de-stress and visualise the connection you have with your baby sending beautiful nurturing pink rays and positive thoughts to surround them*

One of my favourite sensory tools at this stage is a harmony necklace or Mexican Bola ball (some of my range can be seen in the toolkit picture). It is a little bell inside a ball worn on a long chain designed to sit at the top of your bump. The sound it makes as you move is designed to be amplified through the amniotic fluid so that your baby can hear it making a direct connection with you. It becomes a familiar sound to them that they will interact with and bring comfort to them when they are born and will also help them to identify your routine.

Your own positive mental well-being is key too and so don't forget some time with your Mentor Mum. Twenty years later and I still have that time with my wonderful friend Laura, not as often as I would like but when we can we put on our walking shoes and power walk (OK quite often it's a stroll nowadays) by the river, but we take it in turns to just let everything out, sometimes just listening and sometimes offering advice – it's our therapy sessions and everyone needs them!

Count the kicks becomes Routine in the Womb

Feeling your baby move for the first time is one of the most amazing feelings that words cannot describe! At first, they are like butterflies in your belly and then they gradually become definitive kicks and movements, usually around 20-22 weeks. Again, every pregnancy is unique so it may be different for you, but if you are worried you haven't felt movement by your second scan mention it to the midwife/sonographer and they can look to see where your placenta is lying as this can affect the movements you feel.

In recent years, counting the number of kicks you feel throughout the day was the way to know your pregnancy was OK – 10 movements by the end of the morning was the recommended number. However, further research has shown that from 24 weeks your baby will start to develop a routine rather than just random movements, which will be a more recognisable routine by around 28 weeks and knowing this routine is the best way to monitor the pregnancy well-being. See the Routine in the Womb Hero section for the full details.

With every mum I have worked with over the past year, 'count the kicks' has not even been mentioned. Sadly, only a few have been told about knowing their baby's routine either. The full NHS recommendations are in the Routine in the Womb Hero section.

If you still want to or find it easier to count the kicks, of course do so; however, just remember that there will be times when your baby is quiet and still and that is normal.

See our campaign blogs for much more information:
www.routineinthewomb.co.uk

Time to let work know

Once you have had your scan and you know everything is progressing well, and more importantly you have an EDD (estimated delivery date) it's time to let work know (if you haven't already – as the first trimester is just as crucial from a managing stress point of view, I would at the very least inform your official line manager, in writing, of your early stage of pregnancy so that any stress at work can be addressed).

They will need to advise you of your SMP (Statutory Maternity Pay) and leave rights but they should also talk to you about your pregnancy at work. As part of our Routine in the Womb campaign we are highlighting the risks to unborn babies from their mother's stress whilst pregnant and stress at work is one of the biggest factors. More worryingly though, scientists have discovered a strong link between job satisfaction and being unhappy or stressed at work to the ability to carry a baby to term or risk premature birth.

This study by obstetricians at Humbolt University in Berlin found that emotional well-being at work can have a more important role in increasing the risks of a premature birth over activities such as lifting and carrying things. Women who are unhappy at work are almost three times more likely to give birth prematurely.

With all of this research proving the links between maternal stress and emotional well-being and the mental health and well-being of their unborn baby and increased risk of premature births, and sadly even neonatal deaths, employers are now more at risk than ever of an employee taking them to a tribunal for failing to manage their stress under their health and safety obligations.

By ensuring employees are made aware of the risks surrounding their pregnancy at work, including managing their stress and working together to alleviate them, should save employers time, money and legal costs. Just as importantly though, it will ensure the well-being of both the employee and her unborn baby.

We have developed two online workshops as part of the campaign, one for you as a mum to know and understand the risks to your unborn baby along with tips on how to manage your stress, and one for employers to provide to you as an employee on your risks at work and how you can alleviate them.

But as a former employer myself, I do ask that you treat us fairly too. Despite what you may think about your employer, an employee having a baby also costs them money too as well as time and effort, so fairness both ways is only, well fair! If you don't work full-time or have a day off, try to fit some of your medical appointments in then instead. Most of all be honest and tell them if anything is worrying you or causing you concern as they can't support you, which is their legal requirement, if they don't know.

Time to bloom

This trimester is usually when you feel your best. I'm sorry if you don't get to 'blossom' as they say, not everyone does, but you will almost certainly begin to look pregnant and hopefully the morning sickness subsides.

I have already stressed the importance of your positive mental well-being but taking care of yourself physically is important too. Carry on eating healthily and drinking plenty of water or green tea. Take some time for a facial or however you like to spend some 'you' time. Your hair and nails usually grow at their best during this time, although you may find they react differently to colouring or polish etc. so always patch test before treatments.

If you haven't already, the second trimester is a great time to start yoga as it will support both your body and mind through the final stages of your pregnancy, just be aware of the changes to your body and don't push yourself.

It is also a time to enjoy and celebrate you, your relationship and your impending journey and if you are thinking of a 'babymoon' – the new trend of a last holiday before baby arrives – now is the time to do it as some airlines will not allow you to travel after 29 weeks.

Let's not forget your partner though (or whoever your support person will be), it is a great time to nurture your relationship and help them connect with baby too as they are in for a bumpy ride as well. The next six months will test the limits of everyone!

The point is, as always, every pregnancy is unique; if you are blooming or feeling like you are on a never-ending rollercoaster, enjoy it to the best you can in the circumstances you face – positivity is a powerful tool!

Bump Day - Second Trimester Babyopathy Toolkit

Oils

Babyopathy Second Trimester Time to Bloom Blend

Is a wonderful blend to support you as you blossom and bloom!

This blend is a perfect companion to your **Bump Day Meditation!**

Crystals

Malachite

Is a beautiful green stone that may have black marbling throughout. It is a stone for protection and strength during this trimester and helps you with the transformation into becoming a mum.

You can add a small polished piece of Malachite next to your bed for this trimester.

Meditation /Sound

Time to Bloom	
My Time to Bloom meditation nurtures you and your baby through this 'blossoming' time, it is about love and nurturing rays of energy to encourage your baby to bloom too.	You can add a small polished piece of Malachite next to your bed for this trimester.
Harmony Necklace	
I love the connection that these beautiful chiming necklaces bring to you and your baby whilst nurturing their hearing in the womb.	Wear throughout the day and take off when it's time to relax at the end of the day.

Heka Balancing

Time to learn!	
The second trimester is a wonderful time to learn the first step of heka balancing yourself (and your partner); you can learn to connect to your baby and send them endless nurturing love and universal energy.	Of course you can still enjoy the benefits of heka balancing for yourself too!

The Relaxed Mum CHECKLIST

✓ **You have your first scan picture so give your baby a nickname, it helps with bonding for both you and dad**

✓ **Have fun connecting with your baby through your joint sensory journey**

✓ **You join our Routine in the Womb campaign and sign up to the RITW – What you need to know Workshop**

✓ **It's your time to bloom – enjoy it however you can**

✓ **Make time for the two of you before baby makes three**

✓ **You have your Second Trimester Babyopathy Toolkit**

Chapter Six
The Routine in the Womb Campaign
- We Have Movement!

Relaxed Mum, Contented Baby!

The Routine in the Womb Campaign - We Have Movement!

Before we head on to the third and last pregnancy trimester I want to talk about my campaign that helps you to know your pregnancy is progressing the way it should.

'Count the kicks' used to be the battle cry for all pregnant mums but midwives are actively saying there is now a better way, as counting the kicks and having subsequent quiet times can cause unnecessary concern, stress and visits to the ante-natal assessment unit.

Instead pregnant mums should 'feel the routine'.

This new way of monitoring your baby in the womb fits in perfectly with my Babyopathy programme and our specific campaign launched in 2017 – Routine in the Womb.

Babyopathy is all about you and your baby's sensory journey and for your baby this of course begins in the womb when all of your baby's senses first develop. So, the focus of this campaign is all about your baby's sensory journey, their response to their sensory bubble (including how they can be affected by your stress hormones) and how you can nurture it for their well-being and routine when they enter the world.

Routine during pregnancy is very rarely spoken about other than 'is baby active?' and maybe 'when do you notice the most movement?' If the answer to these questions is 'baby's movements keep me awake all night' then it is quite likely your baby will be up all night and sleeping all day when they arrive, but it's not always the case. However, we can nurture that and work on a routine that is more conducive to 'day and night' and 'bedtime' when they arrive.

First though is the most important part of my Routine in the Womb campaign, focusing on knowing your baby's routine, and in particular their pattern of movements, as it is this that you should be aware of and any subtle changes as this is how you follow your baby's well-being.

Once you reach 24 weeks, with most pregnancies you can feel definite movements and kicks and those movements will start to strengthen and form a routine for your baby in the womb. At first it will be hard and it will seem like they do different things on different days but they should settle (every baby is unique though). This of course does depend on where your placenta is lying and an anterior placenta for example will make it more difficult to feel movements and a discernable routine. In these cases, you should still look to feel and count definitive movements during the day.

From about around 28 weeks, every pregnancy is unique remember, your baby will begin to develop a discernible routine or pattern of movement and rest. This will be unique to you and your baby and can be influenced by what your own normal routine is – when you are active or sitting still or relaxing etc.

Take the time to notice how your baby reacts to you and your normal routine. For example, does baby relax and have less movement if you relax or do they see it as an opportunity to finally get their wiggle on? Or, do you find that if you are busy and rushing around that they too become active or does all the movement 'rock' them to sleep? Knowing how your baby reacts to you and your routine is what matters – not what someone else's baby does.

Get to know the nuances of your baby's habits and understand their routine. This is important for two reasons:

✿ *Most importantly, if there is a change to this usual routine without explanation, speak to your midwife or MAU (Maternity Assessment Unit)*

✿ *You can use their reactions to your behaviour as a way to nurture their routine into a more suitable routine for once they arrive!*

So, to re-cap, as you enter the last trimester, count the kicks becomes feel the Routine in the Womb – learn your baby's usual routine in the womb and what affects it – if you go to the gym are they more active or if you have a warm bath do they sleep etc.? There will be certain times of the day (or night) that your baby will be more active and times when they will not seem to move at all and are most likely sleeping. Remember, every baby and pregnancy is unique so don't compare to others, just learn your own baby's patterns.

If the routine that you know is usual for your baby changes suddenly then raise this with your midwife.

If you are concerned you haven't felt movements or your baby's usual routine has changed unexpectedly, try some of the old favourites to get baby moving:

✓ *Eat something – your body makes noises as it digests which should wake baby up if they are sleeping*

✓ *Drink a glass of cola – not usually recommended during pregnancy but in this instance the rush of caffeine will also make baby a bit more lively*

✓ *Put some music on and have a little boogie – the endorphins will filter through to baby and they will hopefully join in*

✓ *You could also just stop and put your feet up – if you have been busy and rushing around you could have rocked baby to sleep for a while*

If you have given these a try and there is no other reason for reduced movement, like you have spent the day putting your feet up after constant rushing around, or you are worried in any way then speak to your MAU (Maternity Assessment Unit – or equivalent, sometimes they are called something different).

Having spoken to a number of midwives recently through my Mentor Mum duties they have stressed that they do not count the kicks any more. They focus purely on your baby's usual routine and any changes to that is what makes them take a closer look, or listen as the case may be!

Information from NHS.UK website:

Do I need to keep track of the kicking?

It is recommended that from 24 weeks of pregnancy you become familiar with your baby's typical daily pattern of movements. It is important for you to know the amount of movement that is normal for your baby. A change in the level of activity of your baby, either reduced or excessively active, may indicate a problem is developing and should be reported to your midwife/doctor.

**Now for a very important aspect of my
Routine in the Womb campaign:**

EFFECTS OF MATERNAL STRESS ON YOUR BABY AND THEIR ROUTINE

Working whilst pregnant years ago wasn't generally an issue as technology wasn't a huge factor and most gave up work at a stage in pregnancy where it was just beginning to impact on everyday life, usually around six months or 11 weeks before a due date.

As we have started to work later and later into our pregnancies and technology has come to the forefront, we now have to take many things into consideration and risk assessments need to be done.

Stress has to be one of the biggest factors affecting the potential development and well-being of your baby at this stage, although technology is not directly attributed to this, or is it?

I don't think I know anyone (of childbearing age that is) that doesn't have a smartphone that is in use pretty much 24/7. More often than not, your work email is also sent directly to your mobile and of course your mobile is just an extension to your office desk. So, advances in technology has made us a 24/7 working machine because who can resist the 'ping' of the email or message coming in – who doesn't 'just check and might as well answer so I don't have to do it in the morning or on Monday?'

Our personal 'down time' has gone, our opportunity to de-stress and relax or to just concentrate on ourselves and our lives and enjoy the world around us. We no longer take time to rest and restore at the end of each day before we start it all over again generally, let alone doing it when pregnant.

All because of the amazing 'must have' latest technological advancement that is the smartphone! So, technology does have a direct effect on our stress levels and maternal stress can have a direct impact on your unborn baby. Stress is one of the biggest factors that can have an effect on your baby's routine in the womb but importantly also your baby's development and well-being. However, this is your stress to be exact, as it is the cortisol you produce when you are stressed that affects baby in the womb.

Over the last two decades or so, our lives, and particularly working lives, have become increasingly stressful. We are stressed before we even get pregnant and we all know the health hazards when it comes to the effects of stress – from the NHS website:

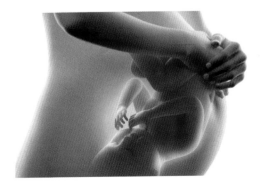

Symptoms of stress

Stress can affect how you feel emotionally, mentally and physically, and also how you behave.

How you may feel EMOTIONALLY	● *overwhelmed* ● *irritable and 'wound up'* ● *anxious or fearful* ● *lacking in self-esteem*
How you may feel MENTALLY	● *racing thoughts* ● *constant worrying* ● *difficulty concentrating* ● *difficulty making decisions*
How you may feel PHYSICALLY	● *headaches* ● *muscle tension or pain* ● *dizziness* ● *sleep problems* ● *feeling tired all the time* ● *eating too much or too little*
How you may BEHAVE	● *how you may behave* ● *drinking or smoking more* ● *snapping at people* ● *avoiding things or people you are having problems with*

All of this and that's *before* you are pregnant! So, can you imagine how much more stressed you will feel once you have to cope mentally, physically and emotionally with your pregnancy too? But how does it affect your baby?

It is well known that a baby's development in the womb can be affected by maternal factors:

Alcohol – *foetal alcohol syndrome*

Smoking – *low birth-weight*

Drugs – *side effects; thalidomide etc.*

However, my theories that the unborn baby could be affected by more than this, by the mother's stress hormone cortisol, began around 2008 due to witnessing a certain baby's journey.

During the pregnancy of Baby A, the parents were going through a very tumultuous relationship that resulted in extremely stressful rows on a very regular basis. This continued throughout the pregnancy and through the baby's first year. From six months old it was very obvious to me that the baby was showing signs of developmental delay and my suspicion was autism. I was unable to observe Baby A on a regular basis, after this however the developmental delays and differences continued and I was told Baby A was eventually diagnosed with autism.

When we are stressed we produce the hormone cortisol which can pass through the placenta and have a direct effect on your unborn baby and specifically their brain development. This is a process called epigenetics.

Sadly, our lives before we even conceive are stressful and this only gets worse once we become pregnant. A certain amount of stress is needed for natural development but when we go through a particularly stressful situation, a personal loss, a fraught relationship or even just pressures at work, this increases our cortisol production and increases the risks to your baby. In both the Before Travelling section and the Thin Blue Line section I have introduced you to the multitude of research that has already been done proving the effects of maternal stress on the unborn baby.

These and other studies have proven the links of excess maternal stress (your stress when pregnant) to:

- ✿ *Potential miscarriage or neonatal death*
- ✿ *Potential premature birth*
- ✿ *Anxiety in babies*
- ✿ *Depression, ADHD and other mental health concerns in babies, children and young adults*

Further studies are being done to include links to autism.

To clarify, your stress during pregnancy can have a direct effect on your baby through the cortisol you produce when stressed that passes through the womb to your baby. This can not only have a direct effect on their development (most importantly brain development in the womb and post-natal mental health well-being) but can also cause your baby to become distressed in the womb causing a change to their usual movement routine. It is vital that you are aware of this information so that you can be proactive and do something about it, learn how to recognise stress and ways to combat it.

Just what can cause stress when pregnant though?

Examples are:

- ❁ *Moving house*
- ❁ *A death in the family or a relationship breakdown*
- ❁ *Already having one or more children and a home to run*
- ❁ *Your usual 'stressful job' – you (and your unborn baby) will feel the effects of this 'usual' stress even more when pregnant!*
- ❁ *Your usual journey into work – especially if using public transport*
- ❁ *A job where you are on your feet all day*
- ❁ *Demands to finish a project or complete a to-do list before you go on leave*
- ❁ *Not being able to take regular breaks*
- ❁ *Working long shifts of nine hours or more*
- ❁ *Pressure to work close to your due date*
- ❁ *Having to train someone to do your job while you are trying to do your job*
- ❁ *The constant buzz of a mobile phone with work email and messages*

Yes, some of these are just 'daily life', but daily life has become so much more stressful and we need to acknowledge that and the increased stress we feel when we then become pregnant.

With these increasing pressures of daily life and in particular stress at work, it is only a matter of time until someone who suffers a tragic loss blames their employer and takes them to court for failing to protect their well-being at work and the floodgates will open.

Don't worry if you are reading this and thinking 'I am already stressed, now what do I do?'

Through our **Routine in the Womb Workshop and Toolkit** you can learn how to combat and reduce the stress and lessen those risks as avoiding them completely is pretty much impossible.

Here are some quick tips to complement the toolkit you can also use to help if you are feeling stressed at work:

1.   A sip and a sniff
Aromatherapy can be used safely during pregnancy if products have been developed especially for pregnancy or you are using recommended oils in a diffuser/inhaler etc. If you have to travel a lot for your work, or use the trains and underground, it can quickly cause you to feel nauseous or faint. I recommend you keep a bottle of lemon essential oil in your bag (as well as a bottle of water with lemons cut up in it to sip) so that you can waft it under your nose to give you an instant mood and energy lift and fight nausea.

2.   Music is food for the soul
Music is one of my favourite sensory 'tools' – it can make you happy, it can make you cry, it can help your digestion and it can help you relax. Setting aside a time in the evening each day to play some relaxing music and just sit and absorb it will help you to de-stress.

3.   Just breathe
Meditation or mindfulness is a growing trend in managing stress that I thoroughly recommend trying to pursue. However, when you are busy and already feeling stressed and pressured some people find it difficult to find the time. I suggest, when feeling stressed and overwhelmed, just take a moment for a few deep breaths – three complete lungs full of air breathed in for a count of five and out for a count of five just to re-balance you.

4. Crystals are a girl's best friend

Move over diamonds, there's a new rock in town! Rose Quartz is the 'mother' of all crystals when it comes to pregnancy. It has a loving, protective energy during pregnancy (and childbirth) and is powerful in healing during stressful times. Many people underestimate the power of crystals, and this is one of my favourites. There are some beautiful polished crystal bracelets available now that will work to combat your stress levels during pregnancy.

5. A walk in nature

Babyopathy encompasses the biophilia hypothesis which is our inbuilt connection with nature that can nurture well-being (and aid development and healing). Just a 10-minute walk immersed in nature, a walk along the riverbank or in amongst trees can have a direct effect on our well-being reducing stress and improving our mood. If the sun is shining you get the added benefit of some much-needed vitamin D as many of us have a deficiency of this essential vitamin.

If you are at work, it is an employer's duty to protect the health, safety and welfare of their employees and they must do whatever is practicable to achieve this – this includes managing your stress when pregnant! But don't worry as we have an online training programme for that too – **Routine in the Womb – Work Wise Workshop!**

The 'revolutionary' part of my Routine in the Womb campaign though is:

Routine in the womb – routine when born

The routine your baby has in the last trimester in the womb is generally accepted as the rough routine they will have when they are born. So, in those final weeks, if your baby keeps you up all night with movements you can expect a baby who is awake in the night once born. The routine that you follow can have an impact on the routine your baby develops as your baby's behaviour in the womb is influenced by any hormones you may produce. If you are very active and even stressed in the evenings on your journey home or attending an exercise class, those hormones could be making your baby more active at night. Our campaign provides mums with ways to nurture their baby's routine through their own routine using Babyopathy influences such as music, meditation and aromatherapy etc. As I said before, it is important to know how **your** routine and daily activities affects your baby's routine so that you can use it to gently nurture their routine over the last six weeks to one that is a bit closer to the one you would love them to follow when they are born.

As always, I must stress that babies are all unique and whilst some may fall into the routine you nurture straight away, others will not. Above all, do not get stressed and do not think you have 'failed' as you have not. You should use all of these tips as things to try to encourage and nurture your baby's own will and personality and eventually you will both get there. Individuality is a beautiful thing, embrace it and nurture that too!

Establishing a routine during the last six weeks or so of your pregnancy that differentiates between day and night is a great way to encourage your baby's sensory journey when they are born. Of course, it's no guarantee that your baby will follow this routine but first and foremost it will ensure you get rest and relaxation when you need it the most because you're in for a fantastic journey and elements will still be familiar to your baby when they are born and make it much easier to influence.

Sensory Chart for Mums

Sound	Sight	Smell	Touch	Taste
One of the biggest tools you can have in your arsenal is meditation! Meditation can be used to alleviate stress, especially if you are working, it can help to combat insomnia and also used during labour.

Music can also be used for relaxation and during labour – generally I would recommend something rhythmic such as spa music or meditation music but in labour your moods can vary so also take something that will 'sustain' you if feeling exhausted or emotional. | Imagery is a powerful thing and I thoroughly recommend finding an image (preferably a nature based one) that you associate with being relaxed: a beach scene, a meadow or even just blue sky and clouds and use it as part of your meditation routine so that if you need to you can take yourself to a quiet place when you need to just by thinking about it. | Lemon: as an oil lemon is mum's best friend when pregnant especially if you are feeling faint – if you can't keep the bottle to hand keep a tissue with some drops on it; lemon is also good for cleaning the air of any smells that may be unpleasant or making you feel nauseous.

For relaxation or when life is stressfull use lavender or chamomile in a diffuser or on a tissue. | Massage is not only great for continuing intimacy with your partner but it is beneficial to you in may ways; to combat stress and stretch marks and to relax – use 10ml wheatgerm as a base oil (always do a patch test first) and add two drops of neroli or orange blossom.

My other recommendation would be yoga but make sure you begin early on into your pregnancy to avoid any strains to your body. | Peppermint: as a tea peppermint is renowned for its abilities to settle digestive disorders so sip to relieve morning sickness.

Ginger: is a super food when it comes to warding of nausea.

Folic acid is a necessary nutrient as are a complete range of vitamins and minerals from a rainbow of fruits and vegetables – this is quite a task and so you can help this by using our Super Sauce recipes later in the book.

Another great source of fruit and vegetable nutrients (27 of them to be precise) I use is JuicePlus in easy to take capsules twice a day – remember it is about healthy living not dieting especially when pregnant! |

Day and night

As well as setting the scene in each room for your baby, one of the most important aspects of your baby's environment is to distinguish clearly between day and night.

Your baby needs sleep, day and night! However, you can't stay at home for the first year of your baby's life so your baby always sleeps in the same place (believe it or not I have read that recommendation in a baby book!). You have a daily routine that you have to do, particularly if you already have an older child, so it is important that your baby fits into that.

So from the beginning, day needs to be day and night needs to be night.

Sense	Day	Night
Sound	Light jazz such as the great Ella Fitzgerald as it is mellow and its rhythms aids digestion.	*No music should be used at night so it clearly differentiates between your normal day routine and night time.*
Sight	Feeding is a great time to bond so either sing along to the music or talk to your baby whilst making eye contact.	*If you must use a light at night keep it as muted as possible to enable you to see but not stimulate your baby. Try not to make eye contact, this is NOT playtime!*
Smell	*We do not include aromatherapy when breastfeeding or bottle-feeding; as your baby is focused on your smell, it is introduced for weaning.*	
Touch	You can cuddle your baby into you, stroke their face or play with their fingers as it's an opportunity to bond.	*Your baby should feel secure in your arms but other than that keep contact to a minimum.*
Taste	*The milk speaks for itself!*	

Surprisingly, reading also begins in the womb. As baby's senses first come alive whilst in the womb so does the foundation for every avenue of development and reading is just one example. By reading to your baby in the womb they will recognise the familiar voice tones and patterns when they are born that not only provides a sense of security and well-being in a sensory overloaded world but will also be building on the foundation for language and literacy as they actively look for you to interact with them.

The indentations that will become baby's ears form around nine weeks of pregnancy and by approximately 17/18 weeks your baby will hear their first sounds. This continues to develop over the next few weeks and so by 24 weeks they become more sensitive to sound. The next few weeks after this your baby will begin to respond to the sounds your baby hears through the womb.

So, as part of the last six weeks of nurturing their routine, choose the same time each day, I suggest early evening when you would be looking to introduce 'bedtime' for your baby, sit comfortably with no distractions and read to your baby. Choose a simple story and one that you enjoy reading as how you read is just as important as reading itself.

One of my favourite first books was *Dear Zoo* by Rod Campbell, not too long and one that is easy to read with enthusiasm using different voice tones. This is important as it is rhythms and tones that your baby will initially recognise not words.

This is why reading begins in the womb. Your baby will recognise your voice tones and the patterns of your voice when reading the story. However, there are many other benefits to you doing this:

✓ *You will be relaxing which means you will be producing serotonin which is well known for the role it plays in your mood and reducing stress and anxiety. When you are stressed your body produces cortisol which can pass through the womb to your baby which can have a direct effect on their brain development. The more you relax, the less cortisol you produce. You can boost the benefits by diffusing the oil from your toolkit too.*

✓ *By reading to your baby your voice tones and patterns will be familiar and therefore comforting to your baby when they are born into a world of sensory overload.*

✓ *By reading at the same time each day (around the time you want to introduce bedtime) you will be creating a familiar routine before your baby is even born, helping you to establish their routine in their first few weeks.*

So, join our campaign to spread the new message that will nurture babies through their sensory journey and support us using the hashtag **#RoutineintheWomb** and join our Facebook community at **www.facebook.com/routineinthewomb**

Routine in the Womb - **Babyopathy Toolkit**

Oils

Routine in the Womb Blend

This is our own branded aromatherapy blend made especially to help you find 15 minutes of relaxation in a stressful world.

Use alongside your Routine in the Womb meditation to boost the de-stressing power!

Crystals

Babyopathy Rose Quartz & Blue Lace Agate Bracelet

Rose Quartz is a must to surround you with a pink bubble of love throughout the day and Blue Lace Agate is the perfect accompaniment to help you communicate everything you need to, especially at work!

Rose Quartz is like a bubble bath for your emotions and worn during the day will help to keep some of the stress at bay.

Meditation /Sound

Routine in the Womb – De-Stress at Work

This meditation has been specially written to support the Time Out oil blend and boost your 15 minutes of relaxation.

You can use this meditation at any time of day to help you through stressful situations.

Heka Balancing

Emotional Balance

Focusing on some emotional balance and stress release during sessions will support this important part of your journey.

The Relaxed Mum CHECKLIST

✓ **You can identify the symptoms of stress and how that affects you personally**

✓ **You have found some ways to help you de-stress each day**

✓ **You have spoken to your employer about managing your stress at work and they have signed you up to the Routine in the Womb – Work Wise Workshop**

✓ **You can identify your baby's 'routine' in the womb so if you are at all concerned you can speak to your midwife or MAU**

✓ **If you struggle to find time for everything, use the Routine in the Womb – 'Let it Go' five minute meditation on our campaign website every day at least**

✓ **You have your Routine in the Womb Toolkit to work on the routine 'after the womb'**

Chapter Seven
The Backpacker
- Third Trimester

The Backpacker
- Third Trimester

Why **The Backpacker?** Because now it's a journey into the unknown for you, where you will need to be prepared for everything, pack all the essentials and have the experience of a lifetime you will never forget!

It's now the start of the countdown to your 'birth' day! However, this is also one of the most frustrating parts of pregnancy – the estimated delivery date or EDD.

From your first scan you will have been given an EDD, based on 40 weeks from the first day of your last period, but it becomes a date you live by, your 'due date'. Your employer (if you're working) will want to know it and plan around it, your midwife and doctor will use it to plan appointments etc. and **you** will use it. Only you will count down the days to it, the anticipation building, and if that day comes and goes it is a huge disappointment (only 4% of babies are born on the 'due date'). I cried because I felt like a beached whale that couldn't even see her toes and I had had enough.

Try not to let it be too much of a 'D' day, just remember it is only an *estimated* due date and a birth anywhere between 37 weeks and 42 weeks is considered 'normal'. This is because a woman's menstruation cycle is not always 28 days with a set ovulation date so your GP/midwife can just give an *estimated* date. It will always be in the back of your mind but it is best to just be prepared and be positive because whatever happens that baby will come out when he or she is ready!

Nutrition

There isn't much more to say about nutrition by this stage other than you can start to increase your calorie intake by around 200 calories a day to support this last stage. However, depending on how your baby likes to lie in the womb and how big and squashed everything is getting, it may start to be uncomfortable to eat a lot. If that is the case then eating little and often might be better for you.

Heka Balancing

As with nutrition, there's not a lot more to be introduced in this trimester. However, one thing I would recommend is for you and/or your partner to learn the first level of heka balancing. There are some huge benefits to this in that if you learn, you can use it as a tool to bond with your baby and send lots of beautiful energy to your baby during the last weeks of the pregnancy. As well as this, the added benefit to your partner learning it is that you get to benefit from this energy too. It can be used for Braxton Hicks too!

Braxton Hicks

Braxton Hicks is the name given to the tightening of the womb that can last for about 30 seconds at any time from early pregnancy and before established labour begins. The womb can continually tighten in this way throughout pregnancy but is not generally felt by mum until the last trimester. They tend to be called 'practice' contractions but are quite different in feel and intensity from labour contractions. Even so, for some they can be painful and there are a number of ways you can get through them:

> **Labour Day** – *our wonderful relaxing oil blend also has pain-relieving properties and so I introduce it with my mums in an inhaler to breathe in as they feel a tightening.*

> **Breathing** – *by taking a deep breath in as the pain begins, even better with the lavender, and breathing out slowly, you*

are increasing the intake of oxygen, it releases endorphins, helps to de-stress and reduce blood pressure and helps to relieve pain.

Turquoise *– this is a beautiful blue stone that can help reduce the intensity of Braxton Hicks.*

Meditation *– if you have been using meditation throughout your pregnancy you will by now find it much easier to find a relaxed state which, of course, helps to relax you and in turn relieve pain.*

Managing stress

Managing stress during this last trimester is again of huge importance to the well-being of your baby. At this stage, we are concerned with an early delivery and managing your stress levels means you are lessening the risk of this. In addition, for all of the reasons I have already discussed, managing your cortisol levels is key to your baby's brain development as there is lots going on in these final weeks. I have written a meditation to reflect this and use the power of positivity to boost it. Plus, it is a great way to encourage the bond with your baby.

Power of positivity

I cannot underestimate the power of positivity at this stage. It will not only help with managing your stress levels but if you surround a thought or situation with positivity it will more than likely be a positive outcome.

The other side to this is self-belief. Believe you can do this, believe you can give birth, believe you will be a relaxed mum or whatever words you want to use. Yes, you may need help, you may need advice and you may need support and all of that is absolutely fine as being a new mum is quite a job – but believe in yourself first and foremost!

Relaxed Mum, Contented Baby

Above all, this mantra matters! The more relaxed you are throughout all of your pregnancy, the more likely your newborn baby will also be relaxed and contented – unless of course they are hungry, tired or need a nappy change – they will still cry to let you know – this is natural and as it should be, but they will settle so much quicker and easier.

Packing a bag!

This section is called the **Backpacker** for good reason as not only is it the start of a long journey but you will never leave the house without a bag that contains almost everything! It does get better, gradually you'll realise you don't need everything but you'll always have a 'mum bag' from now on.

With your hospital bag, it's good to have it packed from about week 32 (I always like to be prepared and it saves panicking later) and just keep it in the car with you, and don't forget that includes having the car seat. I have seen bags ranging from small handbag size right up to a full check-in size suitcase – but I don't think you need to go that far. I have quoted packing newborn size, but your midwife will be giving you an idea if you are having a bigger baby and so can pack accordingly; some are still caught out by the size of their baby when born though, so no need for a shopping frenzy before they're here.

Most important things are a couple of newborn size vests and baby-grows (your hospital stay may only be a few hours but you never know and first poops can go everywhere!) and the trend now is to have a little 'going home' outfit, kind of cute I have to say. Please include a hat though, whatever the weather, as your baby loses most of their heat through their head. A blanket to wrap them in the all-important car seat is also advised and do remember, no coats in a car seat, the straps don't do their job properly.

Now of course you need to think about buying and packing some newborn nappies, baby wipes or cotton wool for the nappy changes and nappy bags, but you just need a few not the whole packets.

Then there's you – as part of your birth plan you will need to think about how you want to give birth and so that leads on to wearing something comfortable and suitable for you to do so. If you want baby put straight on to your skin, this is hugely beneficial to baby, then something opening at the front will be helpful, similarly if you want to let them breastfeed straight away too. You will just want to soak up those first moments and not be bothered with having to change your clothes.

You will however need and want something clean and comfortable to go home in – please remember your bump does not miraculously disappear, that takes weeks/months (or can, not everyone is the same). I have never understood how anyone can make the comment 'Oh you still look pregnant' after a baby has been born; everything has been stretched to its capacity and needs time to adjust and settle back to where it was, inside as well as out. So, pack something that is still going to accommodate a bump and not pull on your belly, it will have been through enough in the past 24 hours.

It's also a good idea just to pack a small travel washbag so that you can have a shower, maybe wash your hair if you need to, and a pair of slippers and a towel. See, the bag is getting bigger already!

Some may want their makeup bag; I would suggest some change for the coffee shop/machine. I would also advise to pack a few snacks for your birth partner/dad and some honey sticks and water for you (I also suggest one of those little lemon-shaped juices too to squeeze into your water – it's the only thing you can pack in advance and know you have with you wherever you go) and of course your Babyopathy Birth Pack!

Finally, whether you have chosen to breastfeed or not you will need some breast pads. Actually, you could need these throughout this whole trimester as you can leak 'milk' before you give birth, but you will definitely need them after. If you are not breastfeeding nature will still do its job and produce the milk so it has to just leak away until it dries up – good breast hygiene is key to stop infection.

If you have chosen to bottle feed, I would advise you make your choice of brand and pack a couple of the ready-made milk and two of the self-sterilising bottles (they can be very quickly sterilised in a microwave) or disposable ones.

Premature birth

I think it is important to talk for a moment about premature birth, because things don't always go to plan. Positivity goes a long way, but it can't prevent everything. I have been present as a birth partner at the birth of a baby girl at eight weeks premature. I had worked with mum all the way through her second pregnancy and she was relaxed and calm throughout. Mum also knew the importance of knowing her baby's routine in the womb, and so when she noticed a change at 31 weeks, she went to the MAU. Following some tests, the hospital identified that she was likely to go into labour soon. This enabled them to give medication to try and prevent it and also medication to strengthen the baby's lungs.

A week later, baby decided she was making an appearance anyway. Mum wanted a natural birth and the midwives were happy to let things progress. We created the environment mum was used to relaxing in with music, crystals, essential oils and a few home comforts and everyone was relaxed and calm, even through the contractions. Six hours after my 4am wake-up call and little baby S was born! She was so settled and calm that the paediatricians were happy for baby to be delivered on to mum's chest, for the cord to stop pulsing before cutting (which I had the privilege of doing) and a few minutes to cuddle and bond before being taken to NICU.

NICU (Neonatal Intensive Care Unit) does not have to be scary, it is after all somewhere that is giving life support to your precious baby, but if you have never seen an incubator, with all the monitors around it, it will be the first thing you see and will be scary. So, here it is, an incubator for you to see and accept as a wonderful place that will keep your baby warm, sustained and nurtured until they are strong enough to come home, so all you need to see is your beautiful baby and know they are in the **best** place. Your baby will need to feel your love and your reassurance, so if you can be calm and prepared it will help you both to still bond, even if all you can do is hold their hand at this stage.

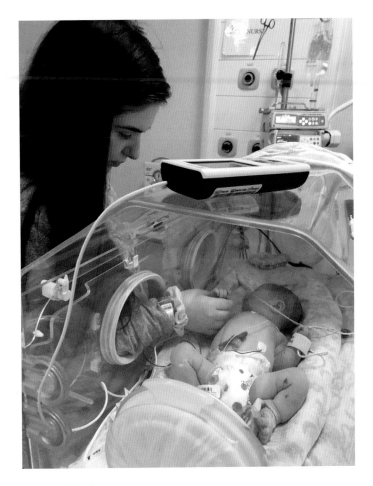

Make a birth plan

Your second most important job during this last trimester is to make a birth plan – you can download a template from the website as a starting point.

You can take your time to think about what is right for you and plan for how you want things, and also a thought for if things don't go completely as planned; very few have a birth that goes exactly to plan and so knowing what you might want to try and include throughout any eventuality is helpful. For example, you may find music very calming and comforting and this is something that could still be included during a caesarean and help you to feel that you still have some control.

The important thing is to be able to have your wishes voiced even if you are not in a state to voice them yourself, you may be too focused on dealing with contractions for example. Discuss your birth plan with your birth partner/dad and your midwife during the last appointments so that everyone is aware.

Nesting!

In today's society, nesting seems to be a thing of the past yet in my opinion is one of the most important parts of this trimester, if not the most important part!

If working, we try to work as close to our due date as possible, when in reality what we should be doing is getting some much-needed rest, taking the time to bond with our baby and 'nest'.

Nesting for me was deciding to refurbish our kitchen at seven months pregnant which included me being up a ladder painting. Not something I would advise, but sorting out your baby's room, preparing the cot or basket next to the bed and taking some time for yourself is essential.

So many mums now report that they did not bond with their baby and it took some up to a year. I think the lack of time to ourselves and no time to nest and form that bond is a huge contribution to this. Once baby is here, there is no time for you and there is also very little time for you as a couple. So, enjoy this time, take a bath with your partner, sing to your baby, read to your baby, nurture the routine you want for your baby when they are here by creating it during those last weeks. Take care of YOU!

'Backpacker' - Babyopathy Toolkit

 **Oils**	**Babyopathy Labour Day Blend** Is a soothing oil for de-stressing and as a pain reliever during Braxton Hicks and eventually during labour.	Use in an inhaler with some deep breathing to help relieve Braxton Hicks and also as practice for the contractions.
	Babyopathy Third Trimester Backpacker Blend This sensuous oil will nurture your last weeks as a couple (or just you is OK too!)!	
 **Crystals**	Turquoise is almost like looking at water frozen in time, it is a beautiful, almost mesmerising soothing mix of blue and white.	You can place a piece of Turquoise in your rose heart necklace if you have one or you can sit holding it in your hand as you take your deep breaths.

Meditation /Sound

The Bond
This meditation is all about the bond you, your baby and your partner (please make this relevant to your own situation) have together and the nurturing energy your baby needs to reach the end of the journey in the womb.

This meditation is great for helping you create that 'bed time' routine you want for your baby when they finally arrive into the world.

Heka

Both of you learning heka 1 to be able to share energy and bond together and as a family is a beautiful way to spend these last weeks of your pregnancy – plus you all benefit from some relaxation and love!

Take some time with your partner to give each other some beautiful heka energy after a bath for example.

The Relaxed Mum CHECKLIST

✓ Take time to make a birth plan, to think about all the choices you would make and let your birth partner and midwife know about it

✓ You should increase your calories by about 200 a day during this last trimester

✓ Don't panic about Braxton Hicks, everyone has them, use them as practice for your 'birth' day!

✓ Managing your stress is key for the development of your baby's brain, again in this last trimester and to reduce the risk of premature birth (and your well-being too!)

✓ Take some time to nest and bond with your baby, it's a crucial part of pregnancy

✓ Take care of you!

✓ You have your Backpacker Toolkit

Chapter Eight

'Birth' Day - I Did It My Way!

babyopathy

Relaxed Mum, Contented Baby!

'Birth' Day - I Did It My Way!

At what point in our past did we stop believing in the power of a woman's body to give birth?

It seems that women have been scaremongered into being completely fearful of giving birth and believing that the only way they can get through the birth is by lying flat in a hospital bed with every drug or intervention possible.

Our bodies are designed to give birth, we have a different physical strength than men when it comes to giving birth, and we have an emotional and mental strength too that gives us what we need to go through the birthing process. We **can** do this, that is a **fact**!

Yes, there are times when medical intervention is needed but it should not be expected, which is where we seem to be right now, and I want to empower women to regain the faith in their bodies, in their physical stamina and in their mental and emotional strength. Believe that you have the power and ability to do it – this is half the battle won.

We have become reliant on medical 'tools' and instead I want to empower mums with nature's tools so that medical intervention and traumatic births are no longer an everyday occurrence. It is OK if medical intervention is needed, it does not make you a 'failure' as a woman or a mum so don't let anyone make you think that. I just want you to believe in you first and foremost, and if anything else is needed, then you can handle it as it happens.

Make a birth plan

It is important to make a birth plan and, as I have suggested, do it at the beginning of the third trimester when you should still be feeling the blossoming effects and are hopefully enjoying being pregnant.

The reason for this is that you have many decisions to make and doing so when you are feeling good and positive is the best time, rather than panicking last minute and making rash decisions.

I suggest you also think about the first few days with your baby too and I have included that in my birth plan, because depending on what happens during the birth, you could be in hospital from anywhere between seven hours after your baby is born to a few days or weeks, and having a plan you can fall back on if you feel overwhelmed or cannot think straight is a huge help.

You can download my Babyopathy Birth Plan from the website.

Choosing a birth partner

This can be a huge bone of contention for many! Dads will now naturally assume that they will be your birth partner, but they might not always be the best choice. Yes of course you want them there (I'm guessing, but it's up to you), but you may also want someone else as your official birth partner. Someone who will be there just for you, will make sure your wishes are followed and you are listened to – your Mentor Mum could be the perfect choice.

How do I know I'm in labour?

Most mums will experience Braxton Hicks or practice contractions in the weeks leading up to their due date. These can last for five minutes or even hours and become quite regular but will pass if you sit and relax, and of course you can use your toolkit to do so.

Your baby's head will drop and rest lower in your pelvis, although again for some this only happens just before birth. However, as your cervix begins to soften and stretch, the mucus plug that has sealed the top of your cervix and protected baby from infections etc. will come away. Sometimes you notice this and it is a sign that baby is not far away, but not everyone sees it.

It is time to contact your MAU when:

- *Your water breaks (not everyone experiences this so don't worry)*
- *Contractions are stronger, longer and regular*
  - *NHS states 'when lasting about a minute and come every five minutes for at least 15 minutes – time a contraction from the beginning of one contraction to the beginning of the next'*
- *Contact MAU before 37 weeks if you experience:*
  - *Your water breaks*
  - *Vaginal bleeding*
  - *Regular contractions as described above*
  - *Severe pain*
  - *An unexplained change in baby's routine in the womb or no discernable movement*

Babyopathy birthing

I know I've probably said it through each stage, and at each stage I mean it, but this really is one of my most favourite stages of pregnancy as far as Babyopathy is concerned as it can play a huge part in the well-being of not just mother and baby but of everyone involved in the birth.

Babyopathy Birthing is one big toolkit I use to nurture you, your baby and anyone else in the room to ensure their focus is on you, your well-being and that of your baby, nurturing their journey into the world! By creating a completely relaxed environment and using meditation throughout the pregnancy, it is very easy to help you enter that relaxed state and progress through labour naturally, without the need of hypnosis or other medical intervention. With all of my mums so far, when we have been able to use the toolkit (in my daughter's case the hospital wouldn't let us, which they have now acknowledged was part of a big failing in her care), it has been the most calm, relaxed and beautiful experience – even if sometimes a little extra medical intervention is required.

Crystals

Whilst you can use some crystals such as Amethyst and Rose Quartz as generalised and universal for everyone, the use of other crystals I would only recommend under the guidance of someone trained specifically in their properties and influences as they need to be cleaned properly and their intentions set. Here are the crystals I may use throughout a Babyopathy Birth with my Babyopathy Mummas:

Peridot: *for someone stuck in the early stages of their labour without seeming to progress I would use Peridot to stimulate those contractions and get things moving.*

Amethyst: *this is a beautiful crystal that you can give as a gift to someone. I use it as a necklace to be worn throughout labour as it soothes and creates positivity and protection, it is a beacon of light and the master of our emotional well-being and healing and shields against negativity.*

Rose Quartz: *I always have in the birth room as it is a stone for unconditional love and emotional balance perfect for a birth but it is also supportive in times of trauma and shock and a birth is a big event mentally, emotionally and physically!*

Moonstone: *is also always in the birth room as it too supports everything that is feminine and maternal and that is of course childbirth.*

Seraphinite: *worn as a bracelet by mum throughout, this beautiful stone fills her body and aura – and that of everyone around her – with calm, joy and healing and ensures the focus of medical staff when they are in the room.*

Larimar: *we introduce once labour is established as it brings confidence and aids communication, something vital for mum now. It also works to alleviate stress and potential post-natal depression.*

> **Chrysocolla:** *is introduced as we enter the actual birth of baby as it relaxes the mind, emits peace, quiet and strength as baby enters the world and gives mum some added strength.*
>
> **Black onyx:** *is also in my toolkit in case labour is taking its toll and some extra strength is needed.*

It is important to understand the subtle properties of each of the crystals you work with and how they can work together. It is also vital that you can recognise when the energy of a crystal is not being effective or may need to be removed, and so although I do sell basic Babyopathy Birthing Kits, the full kit is only used by a trained consultant.

Heka Balancing

Heka is a powerful tool to bring calm and nurturing energy throughout every stage of pregnancy, and in particular to mum and baby just after the birth to ease them both through the transition into their new worlds and bring some emotional and psychological balance to them both.

At birth, or shortly after, as heka practitioners we have to nurture baby's connections in the physical world. A baby's aura almost knows no bounds when they are born as it opens as they enter the physical world to enable the connection to mum in the physical world to take place; you will notice a baby can seem sound asleep but if you even enter the room they will sense it. This of course means that their subtle energy system is susceptible to a multitude of energies and influences during their first days. Therefore, before too many people visit and handle a newborn baby it is very important to close the baby's aura.

We do this during a short first connection heka balancing treatment, as soon after birth as possible. We then connect baby to their **earth star chakra**, which allows them to draw energy from the earth that will support their chakra journey as they fully activate. This does not all happen at once but over their entire childhood.

Music, Meditation and Movement

I love the power of both music and meditation and during the birth is no exception. A playlist of your favourite music is a must and I would prepare both stimulating and uplifting music to get you through the early stages – and to have a boogie which can help get things progressing and then also something relaxing for when things get serious and you need some inner strength.

If you have been using the birth preparation meditation in the final weeks it can really help you in the final stage when every ounce of mental and physical strength is needed, and yet you want to be present and immersed in the birth rather than 'spaced out' as some mums have described.

Movement is also a great tool during your labour stage as it can help baby to work their way down the birth canal (gravity plays a part!). A gentle boogie/wiggle to some uplifting music whilst dilating will not only help this to progress but it will also help your emotional well-being getting through the contractions.

Just as movement is important during labour, position to give birth can also be key in how things progress. Our natural position to give birth is actually to squat as it helps with pelvis position and to push baby out. If exhausted and/or struggling to maintain this position, try being on all fours or leaning over a yoga ball. Everyone finds the position that is comfortable for them, unless of course intervention is needed and then it can be taken out of your hands; the important thing at this stage is to just do what is needed for baby to get here safely.

Aromatherapy

One of the most powerful tools in Babyopathy Birthing is aromatherapy. Again, I would say you can generalise the use of lavender as it calms the mind, especially through the shock of childbirth, and our Birth Day blend as it has been especially made for this purpose, but anything else should be used by a trained consultant.

Here's some of my Birthing Toolkit:

Labour Day: *our wonderful relaxing oil blend also has pain-relieving properties and so I introduce it with my mums in an inhaler to breathe in as they feel the beginning of each contraction. Hold it (or get your birth partner to) right under your nose so that you can take nice big deep breaths in through your nose and out through your mouth during each contraction, allowing the olfactory system to be bathed in this beautiful blend for relaxation and pain relief. Take it away as the contraction subsides. All of my mums have managed their labour this way and only moving on to gas and air during the last final intense stage of delivery.*

Birth Day Blend: *is a pre-mixed blend in a massage oil so that you, or your birth partner, can rub your belly during labour to help it progress and give a little extra pain relief. It can also be used from 28 weeks to help to prepare and support your uterus and encourage dilation if labour has stalled. You can also enjoy a nurturing bath with this blend in some bath oil to kick start it again naturally.*

This blend can be inhaled directly, only in the final stages of labour, to help bring a euphoric state at the point of birth instead of a traumatic or potentially expletive laden one – it has been known!

Peppermint: *is also in the toolkit as it is the friend to the mum who is feeling nauseous or in need of some energy.*

NB: If you choose to progress to using gas and air I would not directly inhale essential oils any further, instead they can be diffused in the room for an ambient effect.

Now, let's talk about your lady bits; an absolute must have for soothing and nurturing any sore bits after birth are 'padsicles'!

Here's what you will need:

✓ *Maternity pads*
✓ *Small food bags*
   (if your maternity pads are not the wrapped version)
✓ **Babyopathy Padsicle Blend**
✓ *Aloe vera gel*
✓ *Witch hazel (optional) in a small spray bottle*

They are very easy to make and will only take you half an hour to make enough to be prepared:

1. *Open up a maternity pad and lay it flat on a cleaned surface.*

2. *Spread a nice layer of aloe vera gel on to the pad.*

3. *Take your Padsicle blend and put the correct amount of drops according to the amount of witch hazel in your spray bottle – shake to mix well and then spray about 4-5 pumps over the aloe vera.*

4. *Wrap back up or fold carefully and place in a small food bag and place in the freezer until you are ready to leave for hospital. By the time you need them they will be defrosted and nice and cool and soothing for your lady bits! When you are home, keep a stock in the fridge – you will want to use them cold, not frozen.*

If you do not want to use witch hazel you can simply add the correct amount of Padsicle blend into the aloe vera gel, mix well and then spread. I however love the added benefits that witch hazel hydrolat brings to them.

Nutrition

Some hospitals do not let you eat during the birth, but keeping hydrated is absolutely vital so break out that lemon water, and a little trick I have learnt over the years is to take along some Manuka honey!

A teaspoon of Manuka honey will not only give you some much-needed energy if you need it, but if you have any sore bits afterwards it has some amazing healing properties too. Apply (and re-apply) after a shower and let nature work its magic.

The Relaxed Mum CHECKLIST

✓ **You have written a birth plan and everyone who needs to know, knows!**

✓ **You are confident to say what is right for you and what isn't**

✓ **You have belief in yourself and your ability as a woman to give birth to your baby and be an amazing mum**

✓ **You are confident to contact your MAU if you have concerns**

✓ **You have your Birth Day Toolkit packed and your Mentor Mum on speed dial**

Chapter Nine

To Infinity and Beyond
-Fourth Trimester

babyopathy

Relaxed Mum, Contented Baby!

To Infinity and Beyond
- Fourth Trimester

I just had to include a Disney reference as you embark on this stage of your parenting journey as being a mum is most definitely 'forever' and your love for your children will know no bounds, as I say to my children (even now they are both officially adults) 'I love you to infinity and beyond.'

Nowadays, we recognise that there is indeed a 'fourth' trimester (I know 'tri' represents three but just go with it, I didn't name it!). In truth, the first six weeks are more crucial in my opinion, especially when it comes to not rushing out of the door and focusing on just you, your baby and your family unit.

When facing childbirth and the first few weeks with a new baby, I was apprehensive even when surrounded by the wealth of experience I had gained during my first three years in the nursery and the knowledge that I had a close-knit family around me, but for many parents now this is not an option.

My second baby, my son, was not an easy baby but then he didn't have an easy journey into the world. I had a very long labour, over 24 hours, and right at the end things took a frantic turn for the worse. His heart rate dropped down to just 44bpm and I was rushed through for an emergency caesarean. My epidural was topped up so I could feel nothing from the neck down, my then husband was rushed in, in full surgical gear, looking just as shell-shocked as I felt. Just as they put the little triangular cushion under my back to lift my belly ready for the surgeons who stood waiting, gloved hands aloft, by the bed, the heart rate lifted a little. The registrar who had made the original call for emergency c-section asked the surgeon if she could have a go at delivering vaginally as I was fully dilated, the surgeon said yes.

All I can say is thank goodness I couldn't see what happened next. My husband said the registrar attached the ventouse suction cup to the top of my son's head, put one foot up on the bed and used her whole weight to pull him out.

I have left out the rest of the gory details as they are for sharing with mums after their birth with a cup of tea and lots of biscuits (believe me we earn them!).

The purpose to this story is that my son was left with a big purple bruise on his head and was traumatised. He was under the paediatrician because of this and his raised temperature for three days. He didn't feed as he was so traumatised, so after about six hours, when I was now back on the ward with three other mums, a midwife just walked over, pulled my gown to expose my breast and said, 'This baby needs to feed,' picked him up, and as she did so clamped her hand around the back of his head right over his big purple bruise. My son started screaming with pain as the midwife was trying to put him on my breast, I was still just sat in shock. The midwife got angry and just put my son in his crib and walked away leaving us both crying. From that moment onwards whenever I tried to feed him he just cried, probably because he now associated the smell of me and my milk with pain.

Why am I telling you my story? Because unlike the stories in many books, mine wasn't an easy, perfect birth, I couldn't breastfeed, I wanted to find a better way for other mums and I hope this will help you.

So many new mothers do not have the support of family close by. Midwives are so stretched that you are lucky if you see the same one twice, and as for health visitors their workload has increased so much a lot of contact is done by completing a form. I am in no way laying the blame at the feet of our midwives and health visitors (my story isn't common), they are simply doing the best they can with the resources they are given, but it's not enough and not consistent.

I know for a fact I would not have survived the first six weeks of my son's life if it had not been for my own mother. Knowing she was there to offer guidance and support was my lifeline, and the fact that when exhaustion got the better of me, there she was staying up all night to do the two-hourly feeds so I could get just enough sleep, thank you Mum!

I had that love and support around me but what happens when new parents don't? How do they know what to do? Do they know to make sure baby's bottom is dry before you put cream on it when changing a nappy? Do they know why a baby needs to wean? All the books just don't seem to give parents this information.

It is about time that parents are given good, sound and consistent advice instead of the latest fad to hit the magazines or the latest directive from Government that bears no relevance.

There is no longer a network of support for new mums; parenting as I've already said used to be passed down the generations and through localised community support but it's no longer there. It seems to have been replaced by a culture of 'follow the next best thing' idealised through books, magazines and the internet.

Well I am here to tell you it's a load of rubbish!

So, forget the books and the internet, what you need is instincts, good old Mother Nature and common sense and that is exactly what Babyopathy is about. Before I go into too much detail, here's the toolkit for when you bring baby home.

To Infinity and Beyond - Babyopathy Toolkit

Oils

To Infinity & Beyond Blend

A beautiful nurturing blend to help encourage sleep at night so that baby begins to recognise the difference between night and day through their senses.

This blend is balancing and nurturing and one drop can be placed on a tissue or diffuser stone whilst you get baby ready for bed – as they get older (over six months) you can diffuse two drops of the blend in their bedroom for five minutes before bedtime to give a light nurturing fragrance. It will also begin to help ease away any stress or anxiety you may have following the birth.

Crystals

Clear Quartz
Amethyst
Blue Lace Agate
Pink Chalcedony
Rose Quartz

Babies are born with their chakras open and so these crystals nurture their energy, their emotional well-being and bonds.

One of the best ways for these crystals to be effective is for you to wear them as a bracelet, that way your baby will get little boosts when in your arms without being overwhelmed and you get to feel their benefits too!

Meditation

Nature sounds

Meditation becomes bedtime music for your newborn and nature sounds that mimic the womb world they have emerged from are most comforting.

Play this music to your baby during their bedtime routine in the evening – even from the very beginning you can choose a time that suits you both to make 'bedtime' just to differentiate day and night.

Heka Balancing

Finding their place in the world

Babies are a blank canvas and have no preconceptions or scepticism when it comes to energy and so just soak up this nurturing energy and help them adjust to their new world.

I thoroughly recommend that your baby experiences heka from the very beginning and even better if it can come from you – heka 1 can be learnt during your third trimester.

The power of touch

The very first sensory interaction you will have with your baby, apart from the visual one of course, is to hold them, touch their face and count their fingers and toes. I can't reiterate the power of touch enough but the average time a baby is physically held between three weeks and three months of age is little more than 2½ hours a day!

Quite often this is due to the increased use of car seats due to their technological advances that mean they come out of the car with baby still in it and slot directly on to the pram frame. This also has a negative impact on their spine and physical development. Factor in the time spent in a cot or pram asleep and there you go. However, I would like to change that, I encourage you to hold your baby at every opportunity, lie skin to skin, look into their eyes and talk to them while you hold them and invest in a sling, not every nap needs to be in a cot.

The most basic way to soothe your baby, make them feel safe and secure is to hold them, skin to skin contact. However, this contact is becoming less and less, and as such we are losing our connectivity to nature and to each other which is contributing negatively to our well-being and mental health.

The current trend of posting on social media from day one with mum and baby out and about in full regalia, especially by celebrities, I think, is putting too much pressure on all mums to do the same and detracting from what both mum and baby really need during the first six weeks.

The first six weeks of your baby's life should be about the two of you connecting, bonding and finding your routines. It should be about nourishing them and yourself, getting sleep when they sleep and finding your way mentally, physically and emotionally as a new mum. Don't be influenced by what everyone else is doing, do what feels right for you and your baby.

I am delighted to share that I am also now a grandmother. I was with my daughter throughout all of her pregnancy and birth, which despite all of my Babyopathy work turned into a very traumatic event due to events at the hospital where she gave birth. In short, I nearly lost both my daughter and my granddaughter, but in a dramatic turn of events my amazing daughter knew what she needed to do and stopped everyone in their tracks to tell them she was pushing her baby out. Little Miss Mia (as she is affectionately called) was delivered on to her belly for a mere few seconds before being whisked off to NICU. Meconium in the womb and the stress she had been under during the labour was taking its toll.

In her first 24 hours Mia struggled, her infection rate was nearly 20 times what it should be and she had to have a lumbar puncture. Sepsis was diagnosed and she was on IV antibiotics for five days. As soon as we could visit NICU, I ensured she received her heka balancing and placed crystals in her NICU cot. Mum couldn't breastfeed and all she could do was hold her baby's fingers to let her know she was there.

The reason I am sharing this is for two reasons. If I had not been there as her birth partner, voicing her wishes and my own concerns, it is likely neither would be here. So again I say, make sure you have your Mentor Mum!

Secondly, despite a traumatic birth and first five days (you can follow Little Miss Mia on Instagram for her full story), as soon as we were able we began using the Babyopathy toolkit to help mum get back on track and relaxed, kept to a day and night time routine, and mum gave Mia as much contact, skin to skin where possible, throughout the day as she could. By the time Mia was three weeks old she was sleeping four hours at night; by 12 weeks this grew to eight hours a night and she was as happy and contented as could be! Yes, it means she has a bottle (mum's milk literally dried up at 10 days so choice was taken away from her) every two hours and hates to be put down during the day because she loves the connections with everyone in the house, but it means she is fully contented and happy to sleep in her cot overnight (now nine hours a night at six months old!).

A relaxed mum with a contented baby!

Breastfeeding

You would not believe some of the things I have heard over the years that parents have been told by midwives and health visitors in order to make them breastfeed:

- ✿ *If you breastfeed they won't get colic*
- ✿ *If you breastfeed they won't have allergies*
- ✿ *If you breastfeed they will sleep better*

What is worse is some of the things I have heard said if you don't breastfeed:

- ✿ *If you don't breastfeed your baby will grow up obese*
- ✿ *If you don't breastfeed your baby will have heart disease*
- ✿ *If you don't breastfeed your baby will catch all of the childhood diseases*

The list for both goes on, and it's all rubbish!

Breast is best, yes, we all know it, it is full of antibodies and provides a certain amount of immunity to your baby and, if you can, you should breastfeed, but do it because it is something you want to do, are comfortable doing and not because you have been pressured into it.

I think it is important not to scaremonger parents into decisions like this and especially seeing as your genetics play a huge part in your future health too, not simply your mother's breast milk.

Strangely though, I have also heard a number of stories whereby breastfeeding mums are also made to feel like complete failures because their breast milk may not be good enough or their baby isn't putting on enough weight. I get so infuriated when rash comments are made to parents and sometimes to very young or inexperienced parents that do not have another support network around them (as witnessed in a health centre with a very young mum of 17 who was left visibly traumatised and still without answers to help her).

Yes, occasionally a baby isn't putting on weight or may not be getting quite enough from their mother's milk and it is right that this should be monitored. However, before making a mum feel like a failure or even scared they are causing harm, look at baby's growth chart; if they are following their own normal growth pattern and no major fluctuations then this might just be normal for this baby – every baby is unique. Common sense plays a huge part in situations like this: is your baby sleeping, are they following a good feeding pattern or do they seem fretful and constantly hungry etc.

If your baby isn't putting on weight, isn't sleeping well or is waking more often, if they are constantly feeding and never satisfied or they are fretful then it makes sense that you may need to question whether they are getting enough milk from you. First of all, don't panic and don't feel bad, there could be many reasons, or reasons why you may not be producing enough milk. What's more important is that, if necessary, you supplement your baby with a bottle of formula. Like all my advice it is always best to not try and change lots of things at once so another reason why it is a good idea to have introduced a bottle from a young age (which you can read about in the next section), so if you do have to introduce some formula, that's all they have to get used to.

A study in 2011 by scientists based at King's College London, The University of Nottingham and the University of Ulm in Germany looked at data from 51,119 children aged 8 to 12 in 21 countries across Europe, Latin America, Africa and Asia and found that babies who were exclusively breastfed for four months or longer were just as likely to develop eczema as those who were weaned earlier. Although the researchers are not disputing the other health benefits breast milk offers, they say that there is only a 'small protective effect' against severe eczema among babies breastfed for less than four months in developed countries.

With regards to your diet as a mum, what you eat (within reason) is more likely to have an impact on you as a mum than your baby, although as I have already mentioned the 'flavours' of what you eat during breastfeeding can influence your baby's taste preferences when weaning. Research suggests that breast milk production is one of those 'Mother Nature miracles' and produces what your baby needs and filters out anything not needed.

I am not suggesting you can now drink coffee all day or can have a few glasses of wine, but like everything that Babyopathy stands for, it's a balance.

A cup of coffee with friends that gives you an hour of mutual support and an escape from the house once in a while, or an occasional glass of wine over dinner with your partner for some well-deserved 'couple' time will do more for your mental and emotional well-being than trying to struggle through being 'perfect' (your body will also process it within two hours and so will not pass to your baby if you don't express or feed during that time). Remember, there's no such thing as perfect! Perfect only happens in films but you've got to love *Mary Poppins*!

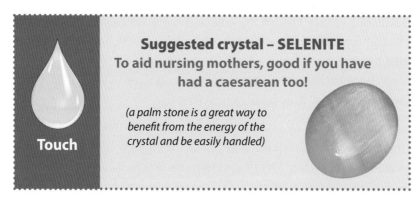

Touch

Suggested crystal – SELENITE
To aid nursing mothers, good if you have had a caesarean too!

(a palm stone is a great way to benefit from the energy of the crystal and be easily handled)

Sometimes though it is possible for your baby to have an allergic reaction to something you are eating; this can just be a one-off meal your baby's digestion doesn't like and tells you through their nappies! However, in some cases it can be more severe. For example, a very good friend of mine breastfed her son but from very early on he started to scratch at his skin.

Over the next few weeks this became much more intense and he developed a rash over his entire body. She tried everything: over-the-counter creams, GP prescribed creams, and gave up dairy herself. Nothing worked.

I gave all the advice I knew: oats in muslin in the bath, not wrapping him up so much as he was sweating and making it more inflamed, and mum avoiding the obvious allergens, but again nothing worked. By the time he was four and a half months old sleep was needed by all.

I advised my friend to introduce a bottle a few weeks previously and he was now able to take a couple of ounces of non-dairy formula prescribed by the GP and he had ravenously consumed his first taste of sweet potato and he managed five hours' sleep. My next piece of advice was a little tough but it had to be tried. No breast milk for 24 hours.

She could express to keep her milk supply and avoid becoming engorged but to give baby only formula and sweet potato for a day – and the rash subsided a little. After the 24 hours she could breastfeed again and look for a reaction in the rash. Proof is in the pudding (or breast milk on this occasion) and back came the rash. So with GP advice it was on to dairy-free bottles for this baby. Most important thing? Baby was fed and no one needed to stress or feel guilty.

Most babies won't have a reaction to something you are eating, but if their genetics dictate they will have an allergy then even when diluted through your milk allergens will cause a reaction.

The main allergens are citrus, dairy, wheat, tomatoes and potato but it is very hard to cut all of that out of your diet, even one at a time, so sometimes the only thing you can do is withhold the breast for 24 hours and then reintroduce to see if this is the cause. That said, my advice is always to eat a healthy balanced diet and you generally are doing what's best for you and your baby.

Something you might want to avoid if breastfeeding though is peppermint tea. Although it is good for digestion and generally would be a good alternative to coffee it can also reduce your milk flow, so avoid it and try some green tea instead.

Our bodies are made to feed our babies and the colostrum that we produce at first is just what your baby needs, so I would always say try and breastfeed if you can.

Sadly, I don't think new mums get anywhere near enough help to ensure a good latch for their baby and there is way too much pressure put on new mums to breastfeed. There is a chemical chain reaction that takes place, stimulated by your baby's cry or rooting, that makes your colostrum and milk flow. For this to happen effectively you should feel calm, comfortable and connected to your baby. Feeling pressured, stressed it's not happening correctly or trying to feed whilst out and about and distracted is not good for you or your baby. 'Brelfies' have a lot to answer for!

When my daughter was born in 1993 I was sent home only seven hours after giving birth and without her having a feed. The midwife just said, 'It's fine, your milk will come in when you relax at home.' I tried numerous times to get her to latch on but it always ended in the same way, with us both in tears. I was told during a fleeting midwife visit I just wasn't producing enough milk and no other advice, so I gave up out of frustration and depression.

When my son was born in 1999 I was determined to succeed in breastfeeding. However, I was not prepared for the distressing birth that left him traumatised with a big bruise on his head and the midwife grabbing it to try and thrust him on my breast.

From that moment on whenever I tried to breastfeed he screamed, associating the smell of me and my milk with pain. Both times after giving up I was made to feel extremely guilty by midwives, health visitors but mostly by other mums even to the point of feeling ostracised. For a long time I felt I wanted to have another baby, not to bring joy to our family but to prove I could breastfeed.

Looking back, what a sorry state of affairs! How sad that my overriding memory of the first few weeks of motherhood is guilt. It is only since getting older and supposedly wiser that I have realised what a waste of time the guilt was. If there had been more help around at that time I would have tried it, but in the absence of that what I needed was acceptance that I had to bottle feed.

It is not the be all and end all if you cannot breastfeed. Yes, it is an important part of your baby's life but it is not the only part. There are many more parts of your baby's life that you can play just as big a part in and influence like weaning and sleeping and health. The time you spend with your baby when they are feeding during the first days and weeks can be the most important you will spend. It is a time for bonding, for nurturing, for instilling security and should be a time for happy memories and a stress-free time. For me it wasn't that, don't let that be the case for you; if you can, breastfeed, if you can't or choose not to, then bottle feed. What's important is that you and your baby are stress free and baby is fed!

Your baby will benefit more by you accepting that you cannot or do not want to breastfeed and relaxing about it than you being stressed and worried about it and, as I have said, your baby will sense this. This just leads to them becoming anxious and then not feeding or sleeping properly and what a vicious circle that becomes.

There are a number of reasons why you may not be able to breastfeed or it may even just be your choice and that is OK. It is also OK not to breastfeed exclusively, to introduce a bottle to supplement if you feel you may not be producing enough milk or give dad a chance to feed and bond for example. What is important is your baby is fed and thriving.

So, my advice to every parent and health professional, you never know someone's circumstances, so just because they are using bottles, do not make them feel guilty, just accept them and support them too. 'Fed is best' is my motto!

Now a little Babyopathy magic for you whether you are breast or bottle feeding as it is important to set the scene whatever you are doing.

Here's a reminder of a little Babyopathy day and night magic:

Sense	Day	Night
Sound	Light jazz such as the great Ella Fitzgerald as it is mellow and its rhythms aids digestion.	*No music should be used at night so it clearly differentiates between your normal day routine and night time.*
Sight	Feeding is a great time to bond so either sing along to the music or talk to your baby whilst making eye contact.	*If you must use a light at night keep it as muted as possible to enable you to see but not stimulate your baby. Try not to make eye contact, this is NOT playtime!*
Smell	*We do not include aromatherapy when breastfeeding or bottle-feeding; as your baby is focused on your smell, it is introduced for weaning.*	
Touch	You can cuddle your baby into you, stroke their face or play with their fingers as it's an opportunity to bond.	*Your baby should feel secure in your arms but other than that keep contact to a minimum.*
Taste	*The milk speaks for itself!*	

Just a little about etiquette…

Whilst I believe every mother should be able to breastfeed their baby whenever they need it there should also be a mutual respect for other people and their personal boundaries.

Everyone has a right to their own feelings or beliefs and so whilst for you it is 'perfectly natural' to 'pop out a boob' in public, it may not seem so for someone else. So, instead of just exposing yourself in public with the attitude 'it's my right', you can be discreet or use a modesty scarf and everyone is respected, but most importantly that bond between you and your baby, the one that supports the flow of milk and encourages a good latch, is kept sacred between just the two of you, as it should be.

Bottle feeding

If you do decide to use formula milk then it is important to research it and not just use a brand because someone else does. Although they are expensive, it is a good idea to try some of the readymade formula first to see if your baby likes it and if it agrees with them.

You wouldn't believe how many gadgets there are on the baby market but you don't really need any of them except a bottle brush and a good steriliser, and even those don't need to be all singing and dancing! A cold water sterilising tank is all you need. I'm not going to waste your time telling you how to sterilise, they give good instructions with the steriliser. But the one thing I do think I should talk about is the different stories I have heard with what you can and can't do with sterilised bottles.

With both of my babies I would place the cooled boiled water in a bottle and the required amount of formula in a sterilised pot. That way when I was out or at night when they woke up I could simply mix the two together and didn't need to heat it as it was room temperature. Now it seems the advice is different, but I do wonder how much of that advice is down to the companies that make the formula not wanting to be sued if a baby is sick. Mine were never sick due to this method but I guess I need to say 'follow the official advice' so you can't sue me either!

One last point about bottle feeding, please please please don't prop a bottle up in your baby's mouth as it can cause them to choke, even when they are several months old. Also, when you're feeding keep the bottle at a rough 45-degree angle and the teat full to reduce the amount of air your baby is sucking in and thus reducing the amount of potential wind.

Breast to bottle

There comes a time when breastfeeding that you may want or need to introduce your baby to a bottle; this may be because you have to go back to work or could be for medical reasons, but whatever the reason it is not always simple.

When trying to introduce a bottle after breastfeeding most people don't realise that it's not just the teat or the taste that is changing but also how you hold your baby whilst feeding.

So, for starters create the familiar scene, wherever you would normally sit to breastfeed and try to position your baby in a similar position. By keeping everything else the same your baby is more likely to accept small changes. Whenever I have had to give advice to parents wanting to introduce a bottle my one big piece of advice is don't leave it too late.

As soon as a breastfeeding routine is established you can introduce a bottle of expressed milk. Whenever you are introducing something new to your baby always do it during the day first. Even though the ideal bottle for your baby to have would be say the 9pm feed, introduce it during the day first, and when you're happy your baby is established with it then move the time.

Try one style of teat at a time; I have always found when breastfeeding too that the NAM brand seems to be the teat accepted the most. However, every baby is unique so the key is to find the right one for your baby.

Do not change everything at once though, don't try and give a bottle and formula for the first time or change teats and milk. Patience is what you need.

Bottles – not just for milk!

The general advice when breastfeeding is that your baby does not need additional water – however, I disagree. Offering a little cooled boiled water when your baby is fretful or has colic can often give them comfort. In fact, boil a pan of water with a just a little fennel, strain and cool it and you have a natural remedy to soothe your baby's stomach or colic. I much prefer the natural approach first rather than an over-the-counter pharmaceutical product, and if your baby won't take a bottle, you don't have a choice.

In addition, when you are trying to introduce a bottle you first have to get them used to the teat, and so using a little cooled boiled water can help you do that without interfering with their feeding routine.

For bottle-fed babies, especially when it is hot weather, you may want to offer them some cooled boiled water to keep them well hydrated in between feeds.

One last comment about bottles: do not be tempted by cheap bottles or teats. Some have been found to contain bisphenol A or BPA which is harmful to your baby. Always ensure any bottles or products you buy for your baby are BPA free.

The dummy debate

I have read so many articles about the use of dummies and indeed there are recommendations from the Department of Health to use a dummy at the start of a sleep period to help reduce the risk of Sudden Infant Death Syndrome (SIDS).

In some respects, introducing a dummy to a breastfed baby ensures they are used to having something different in their mouth and less likely to refuse a bottle when you need to introduce one. Here, advice differs with some saying that you should ensure the baby's feeding pattern and latching on is well established before introducing a dummy, so after about a month old, but by then they are not likely to accept a dummy anyway.

With any baby, a dummy can be a way of helping to pacify themselves and some believe it encourages a better sleep routine. With anything you want to introduce with your baby it is better to start when they are born and then it all becomes a natural part of their routine.

However, as with any debate there are always the arguments against and the biggest one has to be using a dummy for too long! You have no idea how much it infuriates me when I see children as old as three or even four with a dummy in their mouth trying to talk. Overuse of a dummy can, and has in many cases I have seen, cause speech delays and even speech impediments (an inability to pronounce all sounds correctly). A dummy should not be used as a pacifier for tantrums either. They should be a sleeping aid to encourage a good sleeping routine and to encourage your baby to settle themselves. Do not put a dummy back into your baby's mouth if it has fallen out when they are asleep.

Either way, if you choose to use a dummy you should ensure you wean your baby off it by their first birthday. My final point, some babies naturally look for something to suck and if you don't give them a dummy they will find their finger or thumb; how easy do you think it is to wean them off their own thumb?

I know that for most this is common sense but it doesn't hurt to point out the obvious sometimes, so here's some do's and don'ts (OK, mainly don'ts):

- ✿ *Never dip your baby's dummy into something (especially anything sweet) and then give it to them, this can damage your baby's developing teeth*

- ✿ *Never use a dummy that is cracked or split – throw it away*

- ✿ *Never tie a dummy in place*

- ✿ *Always wean a baby off a dummy by the age of one; if they can ask for it, they are too old for it and it will be harming their natural development*

Baby's first instincts

The great thing about babies, human or from the animal world, is that they are all born with basic instincts. Humans may not have the instincts to stand and be running in the first few hours but they certainly have the ability to let you know when they need something!

Almost instantly (if a birth has not been too traumatic) your baby's rooting reflex may kick in and they will turn their head looking for your breast. They will turn their head if you brush their cheek and more often than not open their mouth wide in anticipation. This may just be a reflex at first but will soon develop into a strong reaction to let you know they're hungry.

Your baby's sucking and swallowing reflexes will have already developed in the womb at about 12 to 13 weeks but they have to learn to co-ordinate the two together to feed so it does take them a while to learn to latch on and feed properly.

The other main reflex you will notice is the 'moro' or startle reflex, which is pretty much what it says. In reaction to a loud noise or being disturbed they may throw their arms and legs out, fingers open wide and maybe even tremble and cry; it is a reflex tested by midwives so don't be alarmed.

Mum's instincts

Just as a baby has instincts, so does mum. For instance, your breastfeeding or 'let down' reflex which is stimulated as you hear your baby cry.

I want to talk a little about the protective instinct.

We all know the term 'mother knows best' and although I think we have become a nation of Health & Safety paranoid, over-conscious parents, I firmly believe that when it really matters, mum does know best.

I am saddened to say that I have seen a number of news reports of babies and children that despite their mum's insistence there is something seriously wrong, are sent home from hospitals and subsequently lose their lives. Yes, babies get fevers, yes babies are sick from time to time and yes babies get rashes, but if you know this is not something normal for your baby and is prolonged and your instinct is telling you something is seriously wrong, then be insistent.

I don't want to scaremonger or send mums rushing to their GP over every little thing, as with anything there has to be a balance. When faced with a fever for the first time or a new rash take a deep breath and relax; most fevers and rashes are just your baby's body dealing with a virus, and if they are old enough some Calpol or Nurofen and plenty of fluids will see them through, but if they persist, seek help.

I think it is important to know that the mother's instinct never leaves you and you should always trust what you are thinking and speak up if you are concerned. Although my son is now almost 18, had I not taken note of my mother's instinct (as well as my 24 years of knowledge) he may not be here today (and today means literally the day I finish this book and send it to the publisher!).

To cut a very long and worrying story short, when he woke up he noticed a sore throat; as there were no doctor appointments available I told him to take some paracetamol and we would get an appointment first thing in the morning. Well, within 12 hours I got a phone call to say his dad, who he had been visiting, was taking him to the local walk-in clinic. I met them there and knew as soon as I saw him he had sepsis.

*Please do take a moment to visit sepsistrust.org and know the signs and symptoms. Sepsis can happen at **any** age, including babies, so know the signs.*

My baby, although now 17, was deteriorating in front of my eyes in the resus section of A&E. I kept saying it started with a sore throat and he had developed sepsis. Well, after six hours, me insisting on more blood tests (and an eventual confession by them of a mix-up with the first bloods) and the fifth doctor who finally looked in his throat, sepsis was confirmed with the source infection being bacterial tonsillitis. However, by this time his heart rate was 120, his temperature was 40° and his blood pressure was 60/40 – we almost lost him to sepsis shock and cardiac arrest. Just in time, after again I spoke up and insisted on the nurse checking his chart as she brought ibuprofen instead of intravenous antibiotics, he was given what he needed and he thankfully started to recover. My son is here today, 24 hours after this happened, because I listened to my mother's instincts and was not afraid to speak up!

Bonding or not bonding

There seems to be so much focus on bonding with your baby. It is assumed, and quite often by mums themselves, that because you have carried your baby for nine months and probably talked to them, felt them move and spent all that time and effort giving birth that you will instantly fall in love and feel an overwhelming bond with them. What may surprise you is that for many this is not the case.

For some, it has been a long painful labour, or a 20-minute, not even time to get to the hospital labour, or even if it is a textbook labour it is still a traumatic process for your body to go through. Psychologically too you are suddenly responsible for the complete well-being of a tiny vulnerable being.

When all you want to do is rest and sleep for a week, you now have a baby to feed and change and care for and boy do these things know how to cry! It quite literally is a shock to your system to suddenly have this new baby 24/7.

So, do not worry, do not feel you are unusual or there is something wrong with you. You may by some miracle be lucky enough to be overwhelmed with the instant bond we all see in the movies. For most of us though it is something that grows and develops as we overcome the shock and effects of the birth and having something that we are completely responsible for.

A little about PND

I have already mentioned post-natal depression in a number of sections but I wanted to give it a section of its own as it is something that some people feel is a taboo and I am here to say categorically, it's not!

Post-natal depression is something that can affect any mother not just first-time mums. It is nothing to be ashamed of or hidden and no one will think any less of you for asking for help. I don't want to make light of the issue and so yes, I am being quite matter of fact in my statements because I want everyone to understand just how important it is to listen to a new mum and to not be afraid to talk about feelings and fears and how help can be offered.

Sometimes you're just tearful and tired; after all, lack of sleep is hard enough when it's just one night but for others it can be more serious, and as I have referred to in a news story, it can have tragic consequences. Unfortunately, you rarely recognise the signs in yourself and so you must rely on those around you to offer the help you need. The key is, if you are feeling tearful, overwhelmed, depressed or even suicidal, then talk to anyone that will listen and make yourself heard. To anyone else that happens to be reading this – a dad, a grandparent or a friend, anyone – it is important to listen, help isn't always asked for directly.

I asked my friend Natasha Crowe who is a qualified Psychotherapist, Counsellor & Easy-Birthing Practitioner who works with women dealing with fertility issues, birth anxiety, HypnoBirthing and PND to share her thoughts:

"Post-natal depression can be both frightening and disabling and over the last decade the number of sufferers, both women and men, has risen dramatically (Ref Mind). This increase could be influenced by many factors including the fragmented communities that many of us live in. Some new parents lack the support of having their families nearer to them geographically and many people may not have family in their lives at all, single parents and young parents have even more factors to consider.

"Other factors such as a sick baby, traumatic birth or feeding issues can add more pressure to new parents. The communities that once helped new mothers in the early days are no longer there, women feel that they have little recovery time and a huge expectation to jump back into their normal everyday routine almost immediately. There is little breathing space between a woman's old life and now the new mothering role. Many new mums find themselves holding a baby for the very first time with little instruction or knowledge on what to do, often expected to achieve mothering perfection as if by magic. We have lost the ability to allow new mums and dads to use their intuition and listen to their baby. It's all about learning to be a parent, which for most is a huge life change and enormous adjustment. When it all becomes too much it is often hard to ask for help; women

feel frightened and ashamed that they can't cope or deal with their feelings.

"PND can happen at any time for women and the misconception is that it starts within the first few months; for some women they can have a huge shift or depressive period within the first couple of years. Recognising the symptoms, emotions and feelings that perhaps fill you with dread at another sleepless night, or a lonely day? Women can display lots of mixed emotions including being tearful, angry or irritable. To be honest, most new parents will feel this way at some point; the key would be if these feelings continued for an extended period of time. Noticing changes in normal behaviour, perhaps hyperactivity, anxiety, OCD, excessive cleaning or overprotective behaviour in some women, may manifest behaviour in different ways in others, by isolating themselves and becoming withdrawn. Remember it's not always the women who appear fed up or depressed who are struggling underneath. Becoming a new parent can involve wonderful moments and great happiness but when the joy is not there then support is needed. PND is not only a distressing condition, it's a serious condition, so the earlier it is spotted the better. For support talk to your GP, health visitor, children's centre or contact a local support group. Remembering that there is help out there, you are not alone and you will get better, just sharing your feelings can really help."

Signs and symptoms of post-natal depression according to PANDAS (Pre- and Post-natal Depression Advice and Support):

- ✿ *Low mood for a long period of time*
- ✿ *Irritable*
- ✿ *Emotional*
- ✿ *Panic attacks*
- ✿ *Lack of concentration and motivation*
- ✿ *Lack of interest in your new baby and yourself*
- ✿ *Feeling alone*
- ✿ *Difficulty sleeping or feeling constantly tired*
- ✿ *Tension – headaches, stomach pains or blurred vision*

❀ *Decrease in appetite or increased appetite*

❀ *Reduced sex drive*

❀ *Feeling useless, worthless and guilty*

❀ *Feeling overwhelmed with situations*

❀ *Unrealistic expectations of motherhood*

More information can be found on the PANDAS website:
www.pandasfoundation.org.uk
Or call their Helpline on 0843 28 98 401

Touch

Suggested crystal – Rose Quartz
To aid calm in cases of post-natal depression

(crystals should be placed in a room where the activity is predominantly taking place - resting)

The Relaxed Mum CHECKLIST

✓ **Don't let others, or more importantly social media, force you into 'getting out there' with your baby – you've both been through an immense experience and you need time to recover and restore yourselves**

✓ **Be proud of YOU – you and your baby are unique and should not be judged or need to compete with anyone else**

✓ **Don't judge anyone else – everyone's journey is personal to them**

✓ **Just focus on you, your baby and your family unit**

✓ **Try different things until you find what works for your unique baby and you**

✓ **Ask for help if you need it**

✓ **You have your Fourth Trimester Toolkit**

Chapter Ten
The First Year

babyopathy
Relaxed Mum, Contented Baby!

The First Year

Neurological pathways continue to develop after birth in response to an action such as a sensory reaction. As a baby gets older these 'actions' become more purposeful, such as reaching for a mobile, and the more the action is repeated, the more secure neural pathway it forms. The mind needs to be stretched continuously if it is to develop and be strong.

This is where the core ethos of the Babyopathy programme was developed from, to expose babies to sensory stimulation through interactive, holistic experiences, using natural and everyday resources, thus encouraging neural stimulation and natural development – baby-led sensory development!

However, as you will hear me say often, there is a key balance as with anything in nature, of ensuring encouragement and stimulation against relaxation and independence – a complete routine.

In order for the brain (neurons and neural pathways) to grow and develop and adapt to any environmental influences, it needs to be exposed to positive stimulation. Negative or no sensory stimulation can have a detrimental effect on a baby's development.

In the words of Dr James Prescott PhD, a developmental neuropsychologist who devoted his whole life to researching sensory deprivation:

> "I am convinced that various abnormal social and emotional behaviours resulting from what psychologists call 'maternal-social' deprivation, that is, a lack of tender, loving care, are caused by a unique type of sensory deprivation, somatosensory deprivation. Derived from the Greek word for body, the term refers to the sensations of touch and body movement which differ from the senses of light, hearing, smell and taste. I believe that the deprivation of body touch, contact and movement are the basic causes of a number of emotional disturbances which include depressive and autistic behaviours, hyperactivity, sexual aberration, drug abuse, violence and aggression."

This is a bold statement for me to include in this book but I felt it demonstrated why I am so vehemently promoting the need for positive sensory stimulation.

Positive stimulation comes from an adult providing the opportunity and experiences, giving the motivation and encouragement to the baby to try, experience and try again. By creating sensory environments that promote well-being and development and by interacting appropriately and creating a balance to allow natural child development and individuality – baby-led sensory development again!

I have become increasingly frustrated over recent years in how child development is regressing, how parents are not given the encouragement, knowledge and tools to help their babies progress. We should be pushing the boundaries and giving children the ability to develop. Instead, more and more news reports are stating how British children are underachieving. So many parents I speak to tell me the advice they are given is to 'let baby do what they want when they want' and are not given any advice on what their baby should be doing for their age or indeed how to encourage it – this is not baby-led development.

Here comes my favourite saying: 'It's not rocket science!'

Babies need sensory stimulation to form the neural pathways that are the basis for their entire developmental path. How we interact with them and encourage them to explore and experiment will shape their future. However, remember my other mantra 'everything is a balance' so encourage and interact but do not be overbearing and give them time for relaxation and restoration.

I want parents to have the tools they need to encourage their baby naturally so that we can stem this downward spiral of developmental regression in future generations and inspire the next scientists (yes rocket ones included!), sportspersons, engineers or whatever they choose to become, just not 'celebrities'!

Sensory development

When I opened my first nursery in 1993, a baby's development was measured by the 'milestones' that had been taught to childcare students for many years. In the years that have followed we have seen many changes from Government that in my opinion have caused developmental achievements to regress.

One of the biggest impacts has been on language development with speech delays resulting from weaning being delayed from four months to the now recommended six months. I will cover this in more detail in the section on weaning.

However, it is not just speech. There is a growing culture of keeping babies as babies for as long as possible instead of nurturing their natural developmental path. When talking about the development of your baby everyone naturally first thinks about the physical side of things – when will they sit up, stand, walk – and indeed these physical skills are hugely important as they are the precursor to cognitive skills, but it is this area where we are seeing developmental delays too. Parents are not being given the knowledge and skills they need to nurture their baby's development and instead seem to be being told to let babies do what they want when they want and as a result delays are occurring.

I want to bring you the knowledge and the tools to encourage your baby as the senses are the key to your baby's complete sensory developmental journey.

For example, to talk a baby's mouth muscles need to be stimulated and this journey begins with their weaning (taste), and to crawl and walk a baby needs to want to move and so we encourage them with visual stimulation (sight).

It's all about the eyes

One of the first things that you want to know about your baby is what colour their eyes will be and when they can focus on you.

A baby's eye colour is one of those beautiful mysteries like 'is it a boy or a girl?' when you are pregnant. They are born one colour yet depending on the genes they inherit from their parents they could stay the same or darken or even change colour completely, and this can be anywhere up to six to nine months old! Now genetics doesn't mean brown-eyed parents will have a brown-eyed baby as we actually have two genes for things like eye colour or hair colour etc. and it depends on which one gets passed on to your baby. I can tell you that the brown gene is dominant, then green and lastly blue (for which you need two blue genes as it is recessive), but as for which ones you will pass to your baby, that is another miracle you have to wait to find out!

As for when your baby can actually focus on you, well you won't have to wait long. At first everything is very fuzzy for your baby and they will blink at bright lights, as would you if you were rudely awoken from your bed, but they can see shapes and the first colour that is familiar and comforting is the apricot hue they would have seen through the womb. Don't be alarmed if your baby squints a lot at first or their eyes roll or one eye seems a little lazy as eye muscle control has not yet developed.

During their first few weeks they can begin to focus to 20-30cm and of course if you hold them close enough they can focus on you, so smile away and experiment with different faces at your baby, they will be highly entertained by your facial expressions.

From six to eight weeks your baby will have gained control of both eyes (so don't worry if you think one eye wanders a little up to this point as it takes a while to control the eye muscles) and can follow a moving object. Although they can now see colour they still have difficulty in distinguishing similar colours or shades, so to stimulate visually go for contrasting colours.

Depth perception develops around four months and because they are also developing control of their arms a great source of entertainment is trying to grasp at anything in front of them including dangling strands of hair, and boy what a grip they have! This is a great age to stimulate with colour and moving objects such as mobiles (safety rules apply though and not at bedtime!) as it coincides with the strengthening of your baby's arms and reaching out to grab hold is great exercise.

Five months old it's time to have some fun! Recognition is developing and your baby will love playing hide and seek, with you behind your hands, with their favourite toy or anything they find exciting at the time. It is also a time that your baby will become a great mimic, so encourage it, smile, pull faces, blow raspberries – anything your baby finds amazing and tries to copy.

By eight months your baby's eyesight is almost as good as an adult's, and as I have already said, by nine months your baby's eye colour will be confirmed, unless they have eyes like me and my daughter that change colour depending on the mood we are in from blue to green to grey!

If you are at all worried about your baby's eyesight at any time then of course you should see your GP; here are some of the things that you should get looked at:

- ❁ *If by six months old your baby cannot track an object with both eyes*
- ❁ *One or both of your baby's eyes wanders a little*
- ❁ *One or both of your baby's eyes cannot move in all directions*

When it comes to Babyopathy, sight can be used to influence in different ways. One of the first things I implemented in my nurseries was colour therapy. I enlisted the services of Britain's most renowned Colour Psychologist, June McLeod, and she worked her magic on my nursery premises. My three nurseries look completely different in their colour schemes, there are no corporate colour schemes for us! The reason? No two buildings are the same, they are different sizes, face different directions and so get different sunlight, and the rooms are used for different things and so it stands to reason that different colours will look different and therefore have different effects in each room.

In addition, June introduced some colour images inspired by flowers and this is a concept I have expanded throughout the nurseries through my research into the human-nature connection.

It was obvious to me that throughout history so many great pieces of art have been inspired by nature: Sunflowers by Van Gogh, The Blue Danube by Johann Strauss II, even the Bird's Nest Stadium in Beijing. Nature is the root of inspiration for almost everything, we just don't open our eyes wide enough to see it, hear it, feel it, taste it, touch it!

So, I naturally made the connection that to create a perfect environment to nurture a child it must be inspired both by nature and incorporate its imagery (vicarious interaction) at every opportunity and the senses to nurture core development.

You can read more about a sensory environment later but for now here is some of the imagery used in the nurseries.

I can hear you, you know...

As I have already mentioned, your baby's hearing begins to develop in the womb by about 18 weeks although at first the clearest sound to them will be your own heartbeat.

As this develops they will be able to hear voices and music, especially rhythms, tones and pitches, albeit muffled; we have all been underwater in a swimming pool and this is what it's like for your baby.

When they are born some things will be familiar to your baby: the tone and pitch of your voice and possibly that of your partner (especially if they've talked to your belly a lot!) and even music that you have played a lot will have familiar rhythms that will be soothing to your baby. Music that has been familiar during your pregnancy can be used once your baby is born as a tool for when you want to settle your baby if they are fractious or set a sleep/bedtime routine. I wouldn't recommend playing heavy metal or rap constantly throughout your pregnancy though as that isn't particularly good bedtime music for babies!

Sound is a wonderful way to stimulate and nurture your baby's development as you don't need expensive toys; for starters you just need you and your voice!

TOP TIP: *Talk to your baby about whatever you are doing and they will love the interaction rewarding you from about six weeks old (but can be earlier) with a smile! Eventually that smile will progress to gurgling and cooing in response as they try to mimic your sounds.*

There are also lots of things around that will amuse and stimulate your baby's hearing with different sounds to listen to:

- ✿ *A ticking clock*
- ✿ *Wind chimes*
- ✿ *Some rice in a plastic bottle (steam sterilised and lid taped on)*

✿ *A book you can read out loud*

✿ *Even your favourite magazine read aloud will amuse your baby and lets you enjoy it at the same time!*

In addition, you can sing to your baby – nursery rhymes or your favourite pop song, it doesn't matter, your baby will love to hear it.

Music plays a great part in your baby's well-being, you only have to think how music influences you to realise it. Music can have an effect on our emotions; we have all listened to sad songs and cried when we are feeling down, sang along to our favourite song that makes us feel good, or even fallen asleep to that wonderful spa music… I can imagine it now! Your baby is no exception! Different music can nurture your baby's well-being and also encourage their development through sensory stimulation. I have even read somewhere that babies as young as five months 'dance' or respond rhythmically to music and seem to find it more interesting than speech!

Music is an integral part of the children's day in my nursery programme, for example:

In the Comfort Zone	*Classical music to calm and welcome (drop off and pick up times with rugs, cushions and familiar toys)*
Meal Times	*Soft jazz to aid digestion*
Relaxation/Sleeping	*Nature sounds (rainforest, whales or the sea etc.) to relax and sleep*
Activity Times	*Anything goes from pop to nursery rhymes (even a bit of Abba!) to encourage the activity or energy levels*

We use music throughout the day to help the babies and children follow a natural routine; can you imagine 60 children all sitting down to eat nicely or 25 going to sleep together? Well they do!

Your baby's hearing will be tested at birth and so it is immediately evident if there is something wrong. However, over time there can sometimes be an issue that develops to affect your baby's hearing.

Both of my children, for example, suffered with glue ear and constant ear infections that resulted in both children having operations to have grommets fitted to drain the fluid build-up. Although with mine it was pretty evident by their raging temperature and red ear that something was wrong, if you are at all concerned you can easily test your baby's hearing by making a noise behind each ear to see if they turn their head to respond to it. If they don't or you are still concerned then of course your GP will advise you.

TOP TIP: *One of the best ways that you can encourage your child's listening is my good old favourite, interaction. If you are out walking and hear a car or a cow in the field or a dog barking in a garden, bring it to the attention of your baby, repeat the sound if you can, tell them what it is. With most developmental actions your baby attempts them because they have seen it or heard it and they achieve them through repetition.*

What's that smell?

With a baby, the answer to that question is more often than not their nappy! However, most people reach for the air freshener without realising that some are not suitable to be spraying around your baby.

A baby's sense of smell is probably the first of their senses to develop and will become highly attuned by their first week of life. Smells can cross the amniotic fluid and pass to your baby and it is well documented that within a few days of being born a baby can distinguish the smell of their mother and in particular their breast milk compared to another.

Aromatherapy is widely accepted now as being able to influence health and well-being and mood, a reason we use it in our nurseries, but it stands to reason that some smells can therefore also have a detrimental effect.

Highly perfumed air fresheners for example, and other chemicals that they may contain, can cause sinus irritation, headaches and even respiratory irritations and so should be avoided wherever possible.

One of the best ways to banish bottom smells is to use aromatherapy oils and in particular, lemon oil. It is a cleansing oil and so works wonders after changing nappies or even to get rid of stale odours after cooking.

Not all aromatherapy oils are suitable for babies and so please do follow the chart below. Although there is no research to suggest once developed a baby's sense of smell gets sharper or indeed weaker, their reaction to smells or sense of preference may be more noticeable around five to six months old.

Oil	Properties	What we use it for
Chamomile	Analgesic, anti-inflammatory, calming NB: DO NOT use during first trimester	We use chamomile during our comfort zone sessions for a calming effect; chamomile is also used in sleep/bedroom areas when children are chesty for its anti-inflammatory properties.
Eucalyptus	Analgesic, antiviral, expectorant	Eucalyptus is used generally in sleep/bedrooms to help clear blocked up noses from colds, it blends well with lavender to encourage restful sleep.
Geranium	Uplifting	Geranium is a great oil for stimulation without creating children that are bouncing off the walls so we use it during activity times.
Lavender	Antidepressant, antiseptic, insecticidal, relaxing	Lavender is the one 'oil for everything' and the only one I would recommend you use in a diffuser from birth; we use it for relaxation times and in sleep/bedrooms; it can also be used for headaches and to help combat post-natal depression.

Oil	Properties	What we use it for
Lemon	Antimicrobial, antiseptic, insecticidal cleansing	We use lemon oil for 'cleaning' the air whether it's from the smells of nappy changing or after meals; it also aids digestion so start to diffuse during the meal. It is also a great pick me up when pregnant, whether to sniff if feeling faint or in water to sip to ward off nausea.
Tea Tree	Antiseptic, antibiotic	Whilst we do not use this in nursery it is a great first aid oil for wounds and insect bites.

> When using aromatherapy in the home for children I would only recommend them for use in a diffuser, in water in a steamy bathroom to sit in (not in the water!) and breathe for a few minutes or on a tissue (out of the reach of the children).

You can widen your child's knowledge even before they can speak by bringing it to their attention when you smell something; your facial expressions and tone of voice will tell them whether you think it is a good or a bad smell too!

TOP TIP: *You will be surprised how your baby can recognise familiar smells and is another great reason to introduce a particular aromatherapy smell for your evening routine too!*

A little about taste

Taste is often overlooked as a sense but again it develops in the womb and through the amniotic fluid that your baby swallows. The flavour of what a mother eats during pregnancy (especially the final trimester) passes through the amniotic fluid to the skin receptors in the nose and mouth and can even influence a baby's preferences when weaning.

I talk a lot more about feeding (breast and bottle) in the Fourth Trimester section, but I would mention now that your baby can taste from the moment they are born. So if breastfeeding, beware what you are putting on your skin and if you introduce a bottle they have to get used to a different taste and texture of the teat as well as the milk inside it. Research has also shown that the flavours of what you eat when breastfeeding are passed through the breast milk and can also influence your baby's preferences during weaning. In other words, yet another reason to ditch the doughnuts and opt for the healthy fruits and vegetables!

Once they start to wean, nutrition plays a huge part in your baby's well-being and development; after all, learning to use their mouth muscles to eat is a precursor to speech development!

There have been many books and television programmes on subjects such as 'we are what we eat' and so we generally accept that food has an effect on our bodies. However, food has an effect on many things, including our mood (you only have to eat that bar of chocolate to realise that!) and lack of certain vitamins and minerals can actually be harmful.

When deciding what to write in this section on taste and also the section on weaning it became evident that it is such an important area, and if everyone likes this book enough I have a mountain of information for a completely separate book on taste and nutrition for babies and families (even on losing weight!) so I shall keep it as simple as I can here.

During my time owning nurseries I developed a specific weaning programme, a baby (under one year) gluten-free menu and a children's (can be used for the whole family) menu. These menus have been carefully set to take into account maximum salt and sugar intake, recommended nutrition intake including ensuring an excess of the 'five a day' but also takes into account my research and recommendations on nutrition including eating a rainbow of foods for the purpose of vitamin and mineral consumption. As you will see when you read the section on weaning, I also recommend withholding certain foods until a later stage to help to reduce allergies, eczema and asthma.

TOP TIP: *I recommend eating a healthy balanced diet both whilst pregnant and also when breastfeeding (and let's face it we should all do it anyway – I curse the person who invented chocolate!) and also to eat a rainbow of both fruits and vegetables each day. It's not as easy as it sounds but my range of Super Sauces (recipes can be found in the book) can help you and your baby do that.*

I like massage too!

I am not an expert on massage and because it can have such a profound effect on health and well-being I rely on a friend of mine who now devotes her life to mother and baby massage to provide the expert information when I need it.

However, what I can tell you is your baby will benefit greatly from a soothing touch and will have an inbuilt sense of security from being held or wrapped in a blanket (beware of overheating though). The importance of touch is emphasised in the Fourth Trimester section.

Massage for babies is now widely recognised as being beneficial for relaxation and sleeping but also has potential benefits for your baby if they suffer with colic or wind, much better to try than medication if you ask me. There has even been evidence to suggest that pre-term babies that are massaged develop quicker and stronger than those that aren't. I firmly believe in the phrase 'a loving touch' and the positive effects it can have on our babies. We also use hand massage in our nurseries for the older children as children that have positive physical contact with each other are less likely to use negative physical behaviour!

One other word on the power of touch that I myself am a huge advocate for is cranial osteopathy. After my son was born, he had a terrible misshapen head from the ventouse birth. He had trouble sleeping, was fractious and cried constantly. I took him to see a cranial osteopath so that he could help to realign his tiny body after such a traumatic entry into the world and it helped almost instantly. Other stories from mums include a baby who wasn't crawling, she would sit up but nothing would get her to crawl. One of our resident cranial osteopaths visited the Babyopathy class she was attending, provided a free treatment and the baby girl's body instantly relaxed and she began to reach out and lean over as if to begin to crawl.

Now I am not saying it is a 'miracle cure' for everything, but if you have concerns about your baby it is certainly worth visiting a reputable and registered cranial osteopath. Whenever a new mum I talk to is having problems with their baby sleeping or feeding for example, I refer them to my own cranial osteopath, Laura Sharman, for me she has 'magic fingers'! Here is what Laura has to say:

"Our babies have been in the safest environment they can be in for the first nine months of their life, then it's birth time. Birth can be a beautiful experience, but sometimes it can be a little rough on our little ones, they can be subjected to huge forces twisting and turning as the uterus pushes them into the outside world, this can mean lots of pressure and stress, especially to the base of the baby's skull. This can leave them with headaches and/or irritation of the nerves that serve the stomach and gut leading to tummy ache and difficultly feeding.

"There may be effects from the use of ventouse or forceps on the temporal bone which houses the hearing apparatus and Eustachian tube leading to blocked ears and subsequent infections.

"There is usually only one way they can tell us: crying, screaming, then perhaps crying again. The cranial osteopath uses her highly developed palpation skills to feel if there is discord in baby's musculoskeletal systems. Using gentle cranial osteopathy baby's stresses and strains can be relieved and removed, safely and effectively, to let our little ones get on with being content once again."

• •

TOP TIP: *Touch is not just about the physical touch from parent to child, your baby has their own sense of touch and sensual receptors throughout their skin. The products you use on their skin, the materials their skin is placed next to and the temperature of their environment all play a part too. Be aware of materials you put your baby in or lay them on; are they likely to make your baby sweat, are they too cold because they have been in the car all night, are they rough and scratchy? All of these things would make us react or shudder so don't be surprised when your baby does too!*

• •

Overstimulation of the senses

I have talked so much about natural sensory stimulation and its benefits but I must make reference to overstimulation of the senses and how this can have a negative impact.

There are some out there who take pieces of research, see its benefits and promote it in a business sense to others who accept the claims that 'sensory stimulation is essential for the development of your baby'. However, what they fail to do is look at all aspects of the research including the detrimental effects things such as overstimulation can have and adjust for it in their promotions.

Although a baby's nervous system is one of the first things to develop at two to three weeks after conception, it is one of the last to reach complete maturity. A newborn baby is therefore born with an immature nervous system and so reacts quickly to sensory stimulation and can easily become overstimulated. This response to sensory stimulation continues to develop throughout the crucial first year of brain development and so it is vital that babies are not overstimulated, something that I have seen in some of the baby activities and classes. Overstimulation can lead to a baby being fractious, crying, rubbing their eyes and generally not responding in a positive way to the toy or activity in front of them, as I have witnessed at some classes claiming to be 'sensory'.

In addition, there are a number of media stimuli targeted towards babies under one year old: television programmes, CD developmental programmes that are said to 'teach your baby to read' or other such visual stimulation. Dr Dimitri Christakis, Director of Seattle Children's Research Institute for Child Health, Behaviour and Development and a Professor of Paediatrics at the University of Washington School of Medicine has concluded that early media and in particular TV exposure can lead to overstimulation and attention problems later in life. In fact his recommendation is that it is inadvisable for children under the age of two years to watch television. I was quite shocked to read that in the last 30 years the average age that a child starts to watch television has dropped from four years old to four months old.

The other aspect that is not taken into consideration by some of the other programmes I have seen is that all babies are unique and some will grow up to develop a sensory processing disorder or be defined as higher on the autistic spectrum, which will not be evident for diagnosis until they reach two or three years old (although I believe the signs begin as early as six months and if more attention was paid to sensory responses by professionals, diagnosis could be a lot earlier).

Overstimulation by television or some of the sensory activities and toys I have seen can create a stressful reaction which can in turn lead to a physical reaction including colic later in the day and have a detrimental effect on development. If a baby is likely to develop a sensory processing disorder later in their life, over sensory stimulation for them can have a huge delaying impact on their development let alone the stress-related factor and of course the physical manifestation on health that stress can cause.

So please, if you take anything from my book remember this: the key to everything is balance! Babies under one year can get plenty of stimulation, as you will read, from their natural environment and encouragement from you or their carer without the need for overstimulating toys, television or activities.

Sensitive periods and consequential paths

Now I know I say it's not rocket science and I do mean that, but I do need to talk about some of the more technical aspects of development as quite often these are ignored and not given the attention that they should.

For every major action of development there is a consequential path of smaller actions that your baby will need to achieve. For example, in order to be able to write when they get to school, your baby will have to develop a number of smaller actions such as the pincer movement and throwing and catching a ball. We cannot expect children to be able to control the small and refined action of a pen if they cannot control the larger arm movements of throwing and catching.

All of these end actions have their beginning rooted in the first year of development and use the senses at their core. So how we encourage and stimulate the senses, especially in the first year, is extremely important.

However, as I say throughout the book, every baby is unique and there isn't 'one size fits all' when it comes to babies, their routines or their development. Although they should all follow the same consequential path, the times that they achieve each action is also crucial.

Old milestones used to be set to quite a rigid marker, for example, a baby would be walking at 12 months old. Many years ago, during my research I realised that although most babies were walking by 12 months, some obviously weren't, but on top of that when they walked had an impact on their future physical development.

This meant there was a naturally occurring timeframe that I call a sensitive period for achieving different actions, for example walking; the sensitive period for walking is 10 months to 14 months. If achieved earlier it is likely that in later life a baby will have a natural ability for physical skills; if achieved later than the sensitive period then there is a possibility a baby may be a little clumsy in their physical abilities but will find they are excelling elsewhere.

TOP TIP: *There are many ways that you can encourage your baby's natural development. The key with everything that Babyopathy promotes is a balance; yes you can encourage development but do not get carried away. Your baby needs sensory stimulation and encouragement and the best way you can do this is through interaction.*

Now it may sound simple but in today's busy lifestyles you will be amazed at how many parents do not know how to interact or play with their children. We seem to have become a nation that relies on technology for many things and entertaining our children is no exception. From musical teddy bears for babies to everything plastic in the toy box and enough TV programmes targeting children to run 24 hours a day on multiple channels.

In a recent survey of 1,600 parents by the toy company Playmobil, more than six out of 10 parents said they only occasionally play with their children and more than nine out of 10 parents buy electronic toys for their children.

Babies don't need technology! They just need YOU!

Whilst there are some great electronic toys on the market and they provide a source of entertainment and stimulation, there seems be a new culture of 'techno-babies' that do not know how to entertain themselves or even play on a basic level by themselves or with their peers.

From the moment your baby is born they will look to you for their basic needs, their comfort and security, so do what comes naturally: talk to them. A baby doesn't care what you are saying, they only care that you are talking to them. They will recognise the tones and pitches in your voice and so repetition is the key here. Find a song, it doesn't have to be a lullaby, that you are comfortable singing and sing it when you want to comfort them or get them to sleep or even when changing their nappy. My favourite with my children was 'You are my sunshine, my only sunshine!'

Whatever you are doing, your baby will be happy if you are talking to them, singing to them and it's a great way to be able to keep them entertained for a few minutes while you do some simple tasks. You will be surprised how quickly your baby will fall into a routine with familiar songs or familiar music for different tasks.

When it comes to interacting as your baby gets older the key is to find a balance between entertaining them and letting them entertain themselves. There is a great training tool that I used to use to teach staff at my nurseries how to interact using both our Babyopathy and Nascuropathy programmes; it helps to understand the different levels of interaction babies and children need to help them develop naturally and to encourage them to explore and be independent.

Like anything I do, I like to make it visual and interactive and so imagine a big 747 airplane…

The Pilot

When you are the pilot you are in charge of the journey, you will take the passengers to their destination. A pilot knows how everything works and the route they should take and takes great delight in telling the passengers all the details: how long the flight is, the route they will take, the countries they will cross, even how high they will fly. The pilot may even give a little weather forecast and a little local information. The pilot wants the passengers to feel completely at ease and secure in their journey and to give them all the information they need that will get them to their destination happy and understanding everything.

When you are the pilot you are opening up a sensory world to your child, you are showing them how they can explore and experience in a safe and secure environment. You are giving them inspiration and motivation but most of all you are giving them knowledge. By doing this you are nurturing their own sense of curiosity and inquisitiveness that will be the basis for their future learning.

Being the pilot you know everything! This is a time when you can have the most fun with language as you can use as much as you can think of to describe or explore or introduce:

✿ *What colour, shape or size?*

✿ *How many?*

✿ *Is it big or small, tall or short, heavy or light etc.?*

✿ *What sound does it make, can you make it too?*

✿ *Is it fast or slow?*

The possibilities for language are endless here but most importantly you can cover every learning area through your interaction.

The Flight Attendant

The flight attendant plays an important role in the journey. Before take-off they give the passengers all of the important information that they may need for the journey: how to use the seat belts, how to operate the doors, where the safety equipment is and how to ask for help if they need it. After take-off they go about their duties in the background, offering help and guidance if needed and supervising any passengers that may not be behaving as they should.

When you are the flight attendant you have to be careful to ensure the right mix of interaction. You are starting your children off with an idea and allowing them to explore and investigate and use their own imagination as to how the activity actually develops. Answer their questions, help if they need it, but if not stay on the peripheral and play along in their way. This allows them to develop as an individual, to explore and experiment but within safe boundaries.

Being the flight attendant you can ask questions to stimulate curiosity and allow the children the freedom to explore and find the answers themselves:

✿ *What happens if…?*

✿ *What else can it do?*

✿ *Why…?*

✿ *Can you do it?*

Allowing children, even young babies, to find out these things for themselves is a hugely important tool for future learning and life but also encourages their natural curiosity for when they are able to experience direct nature interaction.

The Passenger

The passengers are of course your children and they are the ones taking the journey. Sometimes they will need the pilot to show them how to play a game or learn something new; other times the flight attendant can start them off on their game or activity and just keep a watchful eye for any help that's needed. Just as important though, a passenger needs to just be a passenger and play with all the buttons and explore the plane, read the magazine and enjoy the ride!

Sometimes your role is to do nothing, and when your children are the passengers, by sitting back and allowing them the space to create their own games, or see how a toy operates for themselves, allows their individuality and self-expression to develop naturally.

By ensuring an equal balance of each of these types of interaction you are creating a balance that will ensure your baby's all-round natural development.

Over the last few decades society has changed a great deal, and for some, family communities that used to be tight knit and supportive through the generations have become spread far and wide. Learning how to interact with children used to be passed down from generation to generation. When I was young we lived near my grandmother and we grew up with my cousins around us. Interacting with babies and children was natural for me, but for many new parents now this is not the case. So, I hope you find my 'airplane journey' helpful in the different levels of interaction your baby will need.

Parents should be given the right information that supports them to encourage their children's development whether they choose to stay at home with them or return to work.

It is vital that babies and children are given the opportunity to develop as individuals, to excel in their own areas of natural ability, but it is also important that they are supported in everything else to ensure an all-round level of achievement. If we don't start doing this not only will we have lost our next generation of great sportspeople or doctors or engineers etc. but as a country we will become reliant on other nations for these skills and will not be seen as an economic and educational world leader any more. We seem to have stopped insisting on boundaries and respect, we no longer let children learn about competitiveness, instead fool them into thinking that 'everyone's a winner' and we do not let children find their own personal boundaries.

So as parents we should be encouraging our babies, we should know what to expect for their development, we should be looking to nurture their natural abilities, but always remember the Babyopathy message 'everything is a balance' and support them in their not so gifted areas too. Just as important though, children need to learn about competitiveness as it is a competitive world we live in; they need to be able to find their own boundaries of fear and courage as it is a dangerous world we live in; and they need to be taught respect and manners as these are a forgotten skill.

Let's get physical

Before we move on I want to talk a little about physical development. Whilst many parents recognise the first few physical milestones such as sitting up and walking, after that the focus seems to move to social skills. However, there are many more detailed physical skills that are extremely important for your baby's development as physical skills are the precursor to cognitive skills.

I have already introduced you to the concept of consequential actions and sensitive periods and now I want you to think about the key to most actions: physical skills.

I don't think I can think of any career that does not involve physical skills of some description. Whether it involves typing on a keyboard, writing a report or something more energetic like riding a bike or building a wall, physical skills are the core to our everyday activities. So, it makes sense that we should ensure that our children start to achieve these actions at the optimum time to maximise their skills in later life.

It's not just everyday jobs that early physical skills affect. Over the past year alone we have heard numerous times that as a nation we need more home-grown sports talent. Whilst the London Olympics produced some amazing moments and great achievements, in many sports there are only a handful of British contenders let alone champions. Babies and in turn children are not being encouraged to develop these skills at a young age when they can be nurtured.

So, yes, as parents we all want to hear our baby's first words but all the physical skills, even the small ones, are ones we need to nurture and encourage as they are the beginning of everything else.

I think at this point I have to say a few words about health and safety. Whilst it is important to make sure we provide a safe environment for our children and we do not put them at risk of harm, it is also important to 'let children be children'. We have become very much a 'nanny state' and health and safety has been taken to ridiculous heights. Children should be allowed to climb trees; yes I know this is about babies in their first year and I am not suggesting this activity for babies, but you get the idea. They can go outside and lie or crawl on the grass and play in the dirt. Our role should be to encourage exploration, yes within a safe environment, but by guidance and allowing them to find their own way, make some mistakes and work out how to do something for themselves will give even the youngest baby a sense of achievement and desire to try something else.

Tummy time

One of the best ways to encourage your baby's physical development is to place them on their tummy; however, due to the widely publicised recommendations to prevent Sudden Infant Death Syndrome, parents seemed to take them literally and stopped putting their babies on their tummy at all.

I talk about SIDS later in the book and the Back to Sleep recommendations are still very valid for when your baby is sleeping. However, it is extremely important for your baby's physical development that they spend time on their tummy.

From about 10 days old, when the cord has dropped off, your baby can spend time on their tummy, only five minutes though when so little and this may be lying chest to chest with you just after a bath or a nappy change and progress to lying on a mat or a rug with you lying in front of them to engage their attention and encourage head control.

As neck muscles grow stronger you can use toys to encourage your baby to use their arms to push up and we all know what this leads to – crawling!

Some babies will protest when you put them on their tummy but do persevere, if only for a few minutes at a time, and build up from there as they get used to it, it is vital for their physical development. As they get stronger you can roll a blanket up and put it under their chest/arms to help support them and this may help to engage them with some activities to keep them interested.

Never leave your baby on their tummy and never put them to sleep on their tummy, and until they have developed their arm strength and the ability to roll over, never for more than 20 minutes at a time.

Most importantly, when your baby learns to roll never place them on a raised surface such as a bed – they are prone to falling off!

A sensory environment

I have talked a lot about sensory stimulation and how important it is for both you and your baby and the best place to start is your surroundings. It is very important to create the right sensory environment in each of the different areas of your home. At my nurseries, we create our own 'sensory oasis' for the perfect environment to support your baby throughout the day – you can do this at home too.

There are huge benefits to differentiating between where your baby sleeps, eats and plays for example and you can use these differences to help set their routine, at the same time nurturing their well-being.

By setting the scene differently using the techniques above you can begin to teach your baby a routine and nurture their natural development just through their senses.

Day and night

As well as setting the scene in each room for your baby one of the most important aspects of your baby's environment is to clearly distinguish between day and night.

Your baby needs sleep, day and night. However, you can't stay home for the first year of your baby's life so your baby always sleeps in the same place (believe it or not I have read that recommendation in a baby book!). You have a daily routine that you have to do, especially if you already have an older child/children so it is important that your baby can fit into that.

So, from the beginning, day needs to be day and night needs to be night.

Nature interaction

Using all of the sensory advice means you will already have created a vicarious natural environment for your baby. However, it is important that we expand your baby's experiences to include both indirect and direct interactions. It is easier than you think.

However, first a little note about the vicarious interaction. As I have shown, it is very easy to encourage this through natural imagery, but as you know from my thoughts on sensory stimulation it is important to ensure *all* senses are encouraged in this way and not just through sight.

Smell and sound are easy: we have flowers, fresh air and aromatherapy as well as music that represents the sea or other nature sounds. Taste naturally comes from the foods that we eat, if you follow our weaning and nutrition programme. Finally, we have touch. Most people naturally think of massage when we talk about touch and yes, massage is the 'sensory' stimulation aspect. However, just as importantly there is a 'nature' aspect to touch and that is through the materials your baby interacts with as well as the shapes and textures.

Remember we are still talking about vicarious interaction, the symbolic or representation of nature so this includes things like:

- ❀ *Lying on or playing with materials such as lamb's wool, silk or something that gives the 'feel' of nature, like grass*

- ❀ *Toys made from wood or grasses such as wicker or even metal (safety rules apply of course)*

- ❀ *Objects for interaction made using natural materials such as water, rice or flowers and leaves*

- ❀ *Objects for interaction using familiar items around them such as a kitchen colander or a wooden spoon or even your curlers!*

One of the most important statements I think I can make for the development and education of babies and children is that you actually do not need *anything* other than the world around you to 'teach' children. You *do not* need expensive toys, you *do not* need lots of resources or even go to brightly coloured soft play centres or play areas. You just need nature and the senses and *you* (or another adult) to guide the way through their childhood developmental years. This rule applies to the school years too.

So, let's move on to the indirect interaction you can provide for your baby. Plants and flowers in the house are obvious choices and letting them have interaction with pets and other animals and places like zoos and farms and gardens and rivers just to name a few are wonderful experiences. Also creating opportunities for experiencing the elements like rain, wind and sun (just make sure you have cream on faces for the wind, sun protection and a warm bath after getting wet). Just remember, you're the 'pilot' here for your baby's journey so have just as much fun as your baby and talk away.

For your baby, direct nature interaction is obviously harder and requires a little indirect help from you to take them into the garden or whatever environment that you are able to. But it is essential to give them the freedom to explore within their own boundaries whilst being aware of their safety and well-being at this age from the perimeter. They can feel the grass with their feet or hands, they can listen to nature, see the birds and insects and so on. All of these experiences are creating a foundation for future exploration as they grow.

Every baby is unique

Before I talk too much more I want to make one thing **very** clear: **every baby is unique!**

There is no 'one routine fits all' and those baby books that try to tell you there is are just taking you and your baby down a path of stress and frustration and possibly depression. There is no 'perfect baby' or 'perfect routine' so for starters throw that idea out of the window!

What you have is some basic rules of do's and don'ts and some basic advice to help you find the routine that suits you and your baby best.

In this book you will find information from my years of research on sleep, feeding, weaning and routines. These are not rules, they are not set in stone, they are my words of advice to help you set your own path. Whatever you are doing it is important that you get the right advice to make an informed choice for what is best for you, do not listen to scaremongering and do not be bullied into making decisions you are not happy with. Most of all, trust your instincts.

When it comes to a routine for you and your baby, most parents simply survive the first few weeks, there is absolutely nothing wrong with this.

● ●

TOP TIP: *Don't panic about the housework, as long as the things that need to be clean are clean (and bottles sterilised if bottle feeding is your choice) then so be it, you won't get a medal for a clean house!*

● ●

There are no right or wrong answers when it comes to what is best for you and your baby, it is a case of have an idea of what you want and trial and error from there to see what works. You may think you have a routine set in stone before the baby is born, you may think you are completely prepared, but babies have a habit of being 'unique' and doing their own thing.

However, don't despair, there are many tricks up my Babyopathy sleeve that you can try to encourage your baby into a routine. What is more important is to not worry about it, what will be, will be. I have seen the most organised woman before their baby's birth completely fall apart when they realise that their baby doesn't fit the routine that the baby book says it should. My advice is just relax and enjoy the closeness you will have with your baby in the first few weeks, revel in those cute snuffling sounds, take time to be skin to skin with your baby and reinforce the bond, and take one step at a time to bring your baby to the routine that suits.

Routines and how they change

There are books that will suggest you should have your baby in a set routine by the time they are six weeks old and make you feel like a complete failure if you don't.

The best advice I can give? Throw that book away!

Your baby is unique, so their routine will be too and during the first few weeks it's pretty much sleeping (16-19 hours a day in anything between 30-minute naps to three to four hours sleep if you are very lucky) and feeding (breast or bottle doesn't mean they will sleep any better at this stage!).

Now, some of these books I refer to that encourage a strict routine can make or break you as a new mum. Granted it does work for some babies but in my opinion that is more luck than anything else. During the first few weeks your baby will let you know when they are hungry, trust me, and it is much better for your baby to feed when they are hungry, especially when breastfeeding, so that they have a good feed of both the fore and hind milk.

A baby is born with natural instincts to feed/be active and sleep in a pattern they will have developed in the womb, which is why it is important to know your baby's routine in the womb and how you can influence it. If you try too quickly to enforce a strict feeding routine from birth which is different from that they have developed in the womb, you are likely to just be making life more difficult and stressful for yourself. My mum always used to say, 'You can lead a horse to water but you can't make it drink' and babies are the same. If you make them wait too long because it's not time for a feed according to the routine you've set then it's highly likely they will become fretful and not feed properly when you eventually give in to the crying. Similarly so, a sleepy baby you are trying to feed just because the schedule dictates will also not feed properly.

You may find that some babies will go through various routines of feeding and sleeping patterns throughout their first six to eight weeks and it is common for them to feed in bursts of every one to two hours and then sleep and maybe have only one feed in six hours, but I'm sorry to say that it might not be at night! But if you keep the same routine you began in the womb, using the same sensory stimuli, they are more likely to settle into it quicker.

TOP TIP: *It takes a while for your baby's biorhythms to settle down and so the best you can do in these first weeks is follow my tips for encouraging the difference between day and night and be patient.*

The other skill that you will quickly perfect in the first few weeks is nappy changing, there will be many!

Your baby probably won't feed too well if they have a dirty nappy but you can almost always guarantee that if you put a clean one on to feed then it will very quickly be dirty and needing a change once they've had a feed. I have found most babies have an inbuilt recognition of a clean nappy!

There's so much I could say about your baby's first few weeks and so many parents ask one common question: 'Is this normal?' The answer is usually yes, but here are some of the more common concerns:

Sweating – *newborn babies have not yet developed the skill to regulate their own temperature and so will, quite often, have a sweaty head; this is normal and may last quite some time (even into adulthood).*

Flaky skin – *nearly all babies will have some degree of dry or flaky skin after their birth due to the difference of environment. I know it is tempting to use those lovely smelling baby products but it may be best just using a simple non-perfumed soap and warm water in the first few weeks until your baby's body adjusts. Another tip is to pat your baby dry after a bath instead of rubbing their skin.*

Nappy rash – *is normal, but different from generally flaky skin. One of the things that annoys me the most for not being taught to childcare students is how to use barrier creams. Most people nowadays use disposable wipes to clean their baby and a barrier cream straight afterwards. Whilst this is completely OK to use there is an important step that a lot of people don't realise: your baby's bottom needs to be dry before you put the barrier cream on; pat dry with a tissue or give your baby's bottom some air time so you are not creating a barrier over already damp skin.*

Other rashes – *there are various types of rashes that are completely normal in a new baby ranging from heat rash (small red spots that may also form a larger red patched area), hormonal rashes (especially if breastfeeding) and these are more like white pimples, and urticaria, small spots that resemble mosquito bites and are completely normal (do not attempt to squeeze these or any other spot on your baby as it can damage their skin).*

The main time to be concerned about any rash on your baby is if it is distressing them and making them scratch or if when you roll a glass over the spot it does not disappear; in these circumstances or if you are at all worried, seek the advice of your GP.

After that first week home, when they are hopefully established at feeding and you have had the chance to recover somewhat from the shock of the birth, you can begin to encourage your baby into a routine based upon their own natural instincts (although if you are unlucky like me and your baby doesn't want to play ball when it comes to telling the difference between night and day, you just have to persevere and go with the flow until they get it) and, in my opinion, now is a good time to think about introducing one bottle if you are breastfeeding.

An ideal routine will completely depend on your lifestyle and family unit. If this is your first baby it is much easier to adapt your life to the routine your baby naturally adopts, but if it is your second or third baby for example, and you have school runs and other commitments, then you will have to encourage your baby into the routine that you need.

All of this may sound like common sense but it is surprising how many new parents become too focused or even paranoid about their baby following a strict routine and end up, like I was, a crying wreck on the floor at six weeks in. I had owned a nursery for three years by the time my first baby was born and six years by the time my second was born and I still felt pressured to have my babies in a set routine by six weeks old. Now I know different – so don't panic, it's normal!

One of the best ways to start encouraging a routine is by introducing the bedtime routine and you can do this from within the womb using the techniques in the earlier sections. Doing this will bring a sense of familiarity to your baby once they are born.

I always recommend keeping rooms separate for different activities so that it becomes familiar to your baby. For example, when you want to encourage your baby into a bedtime routine always move to the bedroom after your baby's bath where you can dim the lights, play some relaxing music (I found my friend's baby fell straight to sleep with my Buddhist chant CD) and keep your voice low. Further advice can be found in the Day vs Night chart.

Who is perfect anyway?

Most generalised parenting books take you on a 'perfect' journey through your pregnancy, birth and baby's development and merely gloss over the things that may be different. After all, every parent wants a 'perfect' baby.

Let me ask you, what is a perfect baby?

My answer? That's easy, **every baby!**

You see there is no such thing as 'perfect' when it comes to a baby because every baby is unique (I'm sure I've said that before!). We all have our subtle differences: eye colour, hair colour, facial features, the list is endless and so every baby becomes a perfect baby in their own way.

We all develop at different rates, some babies are on the 50th percentile, others are not, some babies will grow up to be rocket scientists (yes, I seem to have a thing for that term) and others will not.

In the past, the world has been quick to label someone that isn't 'normal' as 'special needs' or 'disabled' or 'autistic'; I completely disagree. There is no 'normal', we are all somewhere on the same spectrum (think of it as one of those music equaliser counters in a recording studio: some buttons are up higher or lower for each of us to give us our 'quirks' but we are all on that scale somewhere).

> ✿ *Everyone has a different physical structure, it is how that structure is nurtured and developed that dictates our limitations and abilities. How we look physically has no bearing on the person we are, that is down to others' prejudice.*

❋ *Everyone is somewhere on the spectrum of life, it is just where on that spectrum that may mean we need to be nurtured and encouraged differently. Take a look at everyone around you and you will see they all have their own little quirks and differences, I know I do!*

❋ *Everyone has something that makes them different. So, if we are all different, who has the right to say what is 'normal'? Perfection when it comes to babies is achieving the miracle of conception and birth, from that point onwards they are unique and that is something pretty special!*

I believe we have gone a little too far with feminism and gender neutrality. We have established babies are unique and that means a girl can be 'pink and sparkly' or a 'tom-boy' or in time find their path is to become a boy for example, and so can boys be boys or play with dolls etc. However, every baby should be allowed to be who they are destined to be without us demonising one way or the other. We are glamorising transgender and too quick to label a child without giving them the space to see just where their journey will take them.

The moral of all of this is 'everyone is unique, therefore everyone is perfect'.

Anyone saying anything different has 'learned' to be prejudiced!

A baby is not born with prejudice, they have to see prejudiced behaviour to learn it.

A baby is not born with hate, they have to see hurtful behaviour and hate to learn it.

A baby is a blank canvas. Your behaviour is what they see and learn.

Don't paint your baby's canvas with negativity, judgment or prejudice, paint it with positivity, individuality and compassion!

Keeping up with the... (I refuse to say the K word)

Now for a little soap box moment! One of the things that irritates me the most in society today is comparison. We have become a nation of voyeurs of others and their lives, we measure our own lives by those of others and quite often those of 'celebrities'. This even extends to pregnancies, mum's weight and more worryingly baby's development. The focus seems to be:

- ❀ *How big is the baby bump? There are even products on sale to 'control your baby bump'. If your bump isn't petite and perfectly shaped then you are not having a 'perfect pregnancy'.*

- ❀ *How much weight can you lose? If you are not back to your pre-pregnancy weight in six weeks then you are not a 'yummy mummy' (who came up with that anyway?).*

- ❀ *How is your baby dressed? Yes, I am serious, this is a major concern especially in magazines and if your baby isn't dressed in the latest fashion then you must be a bad mother!*

- ❀ *Do you have the latest 'must have' pram? Don't you dare go out of that door if it's not the latest designer name, oh the shame!*

- ❀ *Is your baby sitting, crawling, talking, walking yet? Forget proud moments, can you capture a photo for Facebook that looks like your baby is the next protégé?*

Yes we want what is best for our babies, yes we want them to develop and achieve, but are designer goods, exhausted mums and constant comparison what is best?

NO!

Stop the torment and put the magazines down, turn off the social media and join my new trend of #mumssupportingmums

Sharing your own personal journey is absolutely your prerogative; just don't feel like you have to 'keep up' with or feel inferior to anyone else!

There is only one thing that is best for your baby, it's not what the latest celebrity is doing, it's not stressing to become a 'yummy mummy' and it certainly isn't keeping up with anyone else, it is quite simply YOU!

Why sleep is important

As an adult, we all know how we feel if we don't get a good night's sleep. The next day it is hard to focus, we are lethargic and more prone to catch the office 'bug'.

It goes without saying that this applies to your baby too but even more so. So much happens when a baby sleeps; research has highlighted the importance of sleep in the development of a baby's central nervous system and in addition it has an impact on their immune system and general sensory development.

It takes quite a time for your baby to be able to filter out the sensory stimulation, especially sounds, movement and light etc. that they don't need to respond to, and this is one of the reasons why establishing a good day versus night routine is essential. It is also a reason to set a positive sensory environment and my argument for not surrounding a baby with ridiculously large images of multi-coloured teddy bears or other such characters, as to process every piece of sensory stimulation, valuable or useless, takes a lot of energy. How can your baby replace that energy? Good quality sleep.

The amount of good quality sleep your baby gets will affect their mood, their feeding pattern, their health, their brain function and alertness, and in turn their development.

You might want to take a leaf out of your baby's book as sleep is the key to your health too!

When and how much sleep is right

Using the advice from the NHS, the approximate sleep recommendations are:

Age	Day	Night
1 week	8 hours	8 hours
3 months	5 hours	10 hours
6 months	4 hours	10 hours
9 months +	3 hours	11 hours

I have completed extensive research over recent years on nutrition, sleep and physical activity patterns, and babies from nine months at my nurseries used to follow routines designed to encourage optimum sleep levels in order to promote brain function and also well-being and development. Taking this into account, my current routine recommendation is to sleep during the day before main meals or feeds and after a period of activity, thus maximising the fuel (energy through food/milk) consumed and enabling the optimum 're-charging'

Ideal nap times become: **8.30am 11.30am 3.30pm**

Ideally the main sleeps would be in the morning and at lunchtime with just a 'top-up' nap at 3.30pm by about six months old if needed to take them through to an ideal bedtime at about 7.00pm. This is of course just a guide and you don't **have** to follow it!

How to encourage sleep

One of the things that I have always found amazing is that I can get anyone's baby to sleep! Anyone's except my own when they were little!

My own children didn't sleep through the night until they were three years old. I even tried the controlled crying with my son and was devastated to find he had been sick in his cot and fallen asleep in it when I went in to check on him when he went quiet, so that book went out of the window (see, we have all had that parenting fail moment!). I tried the radio but found he would just 'talk' back to the DJ. Oh, how I wish I had done all this research before I had my own children!

I have already given you the day versus night tips and these are so important as you really want your baby to know that night time is for sleeping not playing. So do not use things such as cot mobiles that will stimulate rather than calm and relax.

The aim is to have a routine, just a simple one, that will become familiar and encourage your baby to sleep. Make sure they are tired out before you start as there's no point trying to get a baby to sleep that's full of energy! When you are ready to take your baby up to bed, say goodnight to whoever is there, reinforcing the fact that 'that's all folks' for today.

A warm bath is relaxing for us so it's a good place to start for your baby, then it's pyjama time and time for bed in the room you have already prepared for 'night time' with low light, quiet music and aromatherapy.

Don't expect miracles that your baby will have a perfect routine from day one; in fact, I would only start your baby's full night time routine when they are six or seven weeks old and established in their feeding. The idea is to stick to the same routine so that it becomes familiar and they know that whatever they do sleep is the ultimate goal.

Touch

Suggested crystal – PINK CHALCEDONY

Great given as a gift to a pregnant mum and placed on the belly – keep near to crib after birth to aid sleep and the connection between parent/baby and the natural world!

(crystals should be placed in a room where the activity is predominantly taking place)

Sleep when baby sleeps

Now after reading all of that you are probably saying, 'Yes but my baby doesn't sleep during the night' or 'I would love to have more sleep.' Trust me, I fully sympathise as neither of my babies slept for more than three hours a night for three years! This is one of the reasons I started my research when my second child was born and slept even less than the first. Can you imagine, just as my daughter slept through the night at three years old, my son was born six months later and he only slept for an hour and a half!

In the first few weeks there is nothing more important. Housework can wait and if you have older children, when your baby is asleep don't try and be Mary Poppins and think you have to do lots of activities with them. Explain the situation and make up some new games or quiet time activities to share or rope in friends to take older children out for you; it is more important you rest until your new baby is in a better routine. Most of all, don't be afraid to ask for help if you need it!

Weaning – What, When and Why

Do you know why your baby needs to wean?

Over the years I have spoken to probably thousands of parents and asked them the question: 'Do you know why your baby needs to wean?' and I am amazed that they still do not know the answer, they are still not given this information. Even more worrying here are some of the reasons that are publicised:

- ✿ *They need more calories*
- ✿ *They can't drink enough milk*
- ✿ *It will help them sleep*
- ✿ *The new super-duper follow-on milks are stuffed full of immune-boosting thing-a-majigs that they need instead*

In the words of a well-known TV comedienne's lovable 'Nan' character *"What a load of old $@*!"*

In actual fact, the main reason a baby needs to wean is for iron. By the time a baby reaches the age of six months they can no longer absorb enough iron from their milk intake, so they need another source of iron. Iron can be directly absorbed from meat but not from vegetables, you need to consume a large amount of vitamin C with vegetable iron to absorb it. However, as you know, you can't introduce meat to your baby as their first foods, it is too hard for their stomach to digest after six months of milk.

If you listen to some health visitors they adamantly state, because of a World Health Organisation directive, that you should exclusively breastfeed for six months and then at six months, when your baby is ready to chew, you can introduce foods. Other fads would even have you skip the traditional introductions of puréed vegetables and go straight on to meat and even forget puréeing too.

I am all for evolution and progression but some things should just not be messed with if it's working! There are many reasons that delaying weaning until six months is wrong, I have touched upon iron but here they are in full:

- ✿ *Babies cannot absorb enough iron from milk by the time they reach the age of six months. You can only absorb iron directly from meat (haem iron) which can only be introduced to your baby's stomach after it has become accustomed to processing more easily digested foods. This can be up to four to six weeks after beginning to wean.*

- ✿ *Plant-based iron is much harder to absorb (only 2-15% of what is consumed), however absorption can be increased by consuming higher amounts of vitamin C at the same time, which for babies is not easy. So, if weaning is left until six months old then iron levels will already be dropping and babies will potentially be becoming deficient.*

- ✿ *You cannot launch straight into weaning by introducing hard to digest foods like meat or by introducing lots of things at once. You need to introduce one food at a time over a day or so, so that you can judge whether it is having any adverse effects or allergic reaction. So again, by leaving it until six months babies will be at risk of iron deficiency.*

✿ *You should begin weaning with puréed food. The reason for this is to encourage the development of your baby's muscles in the face so that you can gradually change the consistency of their food from mushed to mashed and then chopped as their muscles strengthen and reflexes grow. Within our nurseries, since the introduction in 2003 of exclusive breastfeeding until six months old, we have seen an increase in speech delays.*

✿ *Weaning is a crucial time for identifying allergies, as I will discuss later. However, if you are introducing everything at once you cannot even begin to identify any potential allergies. With more and more children being identified as having allergies it is crucial to try and prevent them, which can be done during weaning.*

Why is it the 'powers that be' that give out all of this official advice do not acknowledge any of these implications or consequences of their changes in recommendations? It has been 10 years since the introduction of six months' exclusive breastfeeding and the evidence in my eyes is overwhelming. We have seen an increase of almost 60% in: (as evidenced by our Local Authority)

✿ *Speech delays*

✿ *Increase in allergies/eczema/asthma*

✿ *Nutritional deficiencies*

Even when reports are undertaken evidence is ignored. According to the report by The Caroline Walker Trust 'Eating Well for the Under 5's in Childcare' there is evidence that the diets of children under five in Britain are:

✿ *Too low in iron*

✿ *Too low in vitamins A and C*

✿ *Too low in zinc*

In addition, some children in the UK have low vitamin D status.

These vitamins are crucial for boosting the immune system, healthy blood cells, growth and strong bones.

So, what do you do? Well it was at the point of weaning my second baby that I seriously began researching into weaning and nutritional requirements of babies and children. As an owner of children's nurseries I knew what a baby needed and when as we had obviously provided weaning foods for the children in our care. However, the more I researched I was surprised at how little parents knew or in fact were told. So, the serious research began.

I looked at nutritional requirements, allergies and the benefits of food combining. I identified a number of foods that seemed to be responsible for childhood eczema and asthma. I looked at introducing certain foods at certain stages of the weaning programme and found that we drastically reduced the number of cases within the nurseries.

During childhood we will develop food habits that will affect us for the rest of our lives. Our health throughout adult life can be dictated by our childhood diet so it is important to lay the foundations from the very beginning. In addition, our tastes and preferences can be shaped very early on in life, led by the example set by parents and carers in the food offered. These early influences mould our whole attitudes towards food and eating. By encouraging and establishing healthy eating patterns from the beginning we can help to promote natural growth and development.

Here is what I recommend to all the parents I now work with…

Around four to five months old (but not before 17 weeks as your baby's gut will not be mature enough to process it; *NB: This is in accordance with the Department of Health - Infant Feeding Recommendations)* is a great time to introduce individual foods. I'm not talking big meals or whole jars of food (more about commercial baby foods later), I am talking about a set programme of introducing tastes and textures to allow both your baby and their stomach time to adapt and to avoid allergic reactions. A teaspoon or ice cube size portion for introduction purposes only.

You will know if your baby is ready, they will most likely be showing interest in your food, they will have control of their head and be able to sit up in a 'bumbo' for example and they will be increasingly hungry. You can increase their milk intake a little or try a 'hungrier' milk if bottle feeding first but if that does not work they are most likely ready to wean. Don't reduce their milk intake at first as you will only be giving them very small amounts to start. The following chart shows the foods we would introduce and at what age.

Twelve Week
Weaning Programme

The following 12 pages contain a weekly progress chart on each page to record the process of weaning your baby.

Please ensure you give clear details on food and amounts consumed including bottles given and initial against entry. If a different food is given please cross out the printed text and write clearly the food given and why. Please also include the current age of your baby on each chart

Baby's Name:

_____

Date of Birth:

_____

Date weaning started:

_____

WEEK 1 - Weaning Programme

Age at Now: _____

		Monday	Tuesday	Wednesday	Thursday	Friday
BREAKFAST		Milk Only **oz**	Milk Only **oz**	Milk Only **oz**	Milk Only **oz**	Milk Only **oz**
		Brand:	Brand:	Brand:	Brand:	Brand:
Details		Time: Initials:	Time: Initials:	Time: Initials:	Time: Initials:	Time: Initials:
BRUNCH		Milk Only **oz**	Milk Only **oz**	Milk Only **oz**	Milk Only **oz**	Milk Only **oz**
		Brand:	Brand:	Brand:	Brand:	Brand:
Details		Time: Initials:	Time: Initials:	Time: Initials:	Time: Initials:	Time: Initials:
LUNCH		Milk Only **oz**	Milk Only **oz**	Milk Only **oz**	Milk Only **oz**	Milk Only **oz**
		Brand:	Brand:	Brand:	Brand:	Brand:
Details		Time: Initials:	Time: Initials:	Time: Initials:	Time: Initials:	Time: Initials:
TEA		Milk Only **oz**	Milk Only **oz**	Milk Only **oz**	Milk Only **oz**	Milk Only **oz**
		Brand:	Brand:	Brand:	Brand:	Brand:
Details		Time: Initials:	Time: Initials:	Time: Initials:	Time: Initials:	Time: Initials:

WEEK 2 - Weaning Programme

Age at Now: _____

	Monday	Tuesday	Wednesday	Thursday	Friday
BREAKFAST	Milk Only	Milk Only	Milk Only	Milk Only	Milk Only
	oz	oz	oz	oz	oz
	Brand:	Brand:	Brand:	Brand:	Brand:
Details	Time: Initials:	Time: Initials:	Time: Initials:	Time: Initials:	Time: Initials:
BRUNCH	Milk Only	Milk Only	Milk Only	Milk Only	Milk Only
	oz	oz	oz	oz	oz
	Brand:	Brand:	Brand:	Brand:	Brand:
Details	Time: Initials:	Time: Initials:	Time: Initials:	Time: Initials:	Time: Initials:
LUNCH	1 cube of carrot	1 cube of sweet potato	1 cube of carrot	1 cube of carrot	1 cube of broccoli
	oz	oz	oz	oz	oz
	Brand:	Brand:	Brand:	Brand:	Brand:
Details	Time: Initials:	Time: Initials:	Time: Initials:	Time: Initials:	Time: Initials:
TEA	Milk Only	Milk Only	Milk Only	Milk Only	Milk Only
	oz	oz	oz	oz	oz
	Brand:	Brand:	Brand:	Brand:	Brand:
Details	Time: Initials:	Time: Initials:	Time: Initials:	Time: Initials:	Time: Initials:

WEEK 3 - Weaning Programme

Age at Now: _____

	Monday	Tuesday	Wednesday	Thursday	Friday
BREAKFAST	Milk Only Brand: oz	Milk Only Brand: oz	Milk Only Brand: oz	Milk Only Brand: oz	Milk Only Brand: oz
Details	Time: Initials:	Time: Initials:	Time: Initials:	Time: Initials:	Time: Initials:
BRUNCH	Milk Only Brand: oz	Milk Only Brand: oz	Milk Only Brand: oz	Milk Only Brand: oz	Milk Only Brand: oz
Details	Time: Initials:	Time: Initials:	Time: Initials:	Time: Initials:	Time: Initials:
LUNCH	1 cube of parsnip & 1 cube of sweet potato Brand: oz	2 cubes of sweet potato Brand: oz	2 cubes of carrot Brand: oz	1 cube of parsnip & 1 cube of sweet potato Brand: oz	1 cube of broccoli & 1 cube of carrot Brand: oz
Details	Time: Initials:	Time: Initials:	Time: Initials:	Time: Initials:	Time: Initials:
TEA	Milk Only Brand: oz	Milk Only Brand: oz	Milk Only Brand: oz	Milk Only Brand: oz	Milk Only Brand: oz
Details	Time: Initials:	Time: Initials:	Time: Initials:	Time: Initials:	Time: Initials:

WEEK 4 - Weaning Programme

Age at Now: _____

	Monday	Tuesday	Wednesday	Thursday	Friday
BREAKFAST	Milk Only	Milk Only	Milk Only	Milk Only	Milk Only
	Brand: _____ oz	Brand: _____ oz	Brand: _____ oz	Brand: _____ oz	Brand: _____ oz
Details	Time: Initials:	Time: Initials:	Time: Initials:	Time: Initials:	Time: Initials:
BRUNCH	Milk Only	Milk Only	Milk Only	Milk Only	Milk Only
	Brand: _____ oz	Brand: _____ oz	Brand: _____ oz	Brand: _____ oz	Brand: _____ oz
Details	Time: Initials:	Time: Initials:	Time: Initials:	Time: Initials:	Time: Initials:
LUNCH	1 cube of green bean & 1 cube of sweet potato Brand: _____ oz	1 cube of carrot & 1 cube of parsnip Brand: _____ oz	1 cube of green bean & 1 cube of sweet potato Brand: _____ oz	1 cube of sweet potato & 1 cube of peas Brand: _____ oz	1 cube of broccoli & 1 cube of carrot Brand: _____ oz
Details	Time: Initials:	Time: Initials:	Time: Initials:	Time: Initials:	Time: Initials:
TEA	Milk Only	Milk Only	Milk Only	Milk Only	Milk Only
	Brand: _____ oz	Brand: _____ oz	Brand: _____ oz	Brand: _____ oz	Brand: _____ oz
Details	Time: Initials:	Time: Initials:	Time: Initials:	Time: Initials:	Time: Initials:

WEEK 5 - Weaning Programme

Age at Now: _____

	Monday	Tuesday	Wednesday	Thursday	Friday
BREAKFAST	Milk Only oz **Brand:**	Milk Only oz **Brand:**	Milk Only oz **Brand:**	Milk Only oz **Brand:**	Milk Only oz **Brand:**
Details	Time: Initials:	Time: Initials:	Time: Initials:	Time: Initials:	Time: Initials:
BRUNCH	Milk Only oz **Brand:**	Milk Only oz **Brand:**	Milk Only oz **Brand:**	Milk Only oz **Brand:**	Milk Only oz **Brand:**
Details	Time: Initials:	Time: Initials:	Time: Initials:	Time: Initials:	Time: Initials:
LUNCH	2 cubes of combo veg: 1 cube of turkey **Brand:** oz	2 cubes of combo veg oz **Brand:**	2 cubes of combo veg: 1 cube of turkey **Brand:** oz	2 cubes of combo veg oz **Brand:**	2 cubes of combo veg: 1 cube of turkey **Brand:** oz
Details	Time: Initials:	Time: Initials:	Time: Initials:	Time: Initials:	Time: Initials:
TEA	Milk Only oz **Brand:**	Milk Only oz **Brand:**	Milk Only oz **Brand:**	Milk Only oz **Brand:**	Milk Only oz **Brand:**
Details	Time: Initials:	Time: Initials:	Time: Initials:	Time: Initials:	Time: Initials:

WEEK 6 – Weaning Programme

Age at Now: _____

	Monday	Tuesday	Wednesday	Thursday	Friday
BREAKFAST	Milk Only oz	Milk Only oz	Milk Only oz	Milk Only oz	Milk Only oz
	Brand:	Brand:	Brand:	Brand:	Brand:
Details	Time: Initials:	Time: Initials:	Time: Initials:	Time: Initials:	Time: Initials:
BRUNCH	Milk Only oz	Milk Only oz	Milk Only oz	Milk Only oz	Milk Only oz
	Brand:	Brand:	Brand:	Brand:	Brand:
Details	Time: Initials:	Time: Initials:	Time: Initials:	Time: Initials:	Time: Initials:
LUNCH	2 cubes of combo veg: 1 cube of fish oz	2 cubes of combo veg: 1 cube of turkey oz	2 cubes of combo veg: 1 cube of fish oz	2 cubes of combo veg: 1 cube of turkey oz	2 cubes of combo veg: 1 cube of fish oz
	Brand:	Brand:	Brand:	Brand:	Brand:
Details	Time: Initials:	Time: Initials:	Time: Initials:	Time: Initials:	Time: Initials:
TEA	Milk Only oz	Milk Only oz	Milk Only oz	Milk Only oz	Milk Only oz
	Brand:	Brand:	Brand:	Brand:	Brand:
Details	Time: Initials:	Time: Initials:	Time: Initials:	Time: Initials:	Time: Initials:

WEEK 7 - Weaning Programme

Age at Now: _____

	Monday	Tuesday	Wednesday	Thursday	Friday
BREAKFAST	Porridge **Brand:** oz	Milk Only **Brand:** oz	Porridge **Brand:** oz	Milk Only **Brand:** oz	Porridge **Brand:** oz
Details	Time: Initials:	Time: Initials:	Time: Initials:	Time: Initials:	Time: Initials:
BRUNCH	Milk Only **Brand:** oz	Milk Only **Brand:** oz	Milk Only **Brand:** oz	Milk Only **Brand:** oz	Milk Only **Brand:** oz
Details	Time: Initials:	Time: Initials:	Time: Initials:	Time: Initials:	Time: Initials:
LUNCH	2 cubes of combo veg: 1 cube of turkey **Brand:** oz	2 cubes of combo veg: 1 cube of fish **Brand:** oz	2 cubes of combo veg: 1 cube of turkey **Brand:** oz	2 cubes of combo veg: 1 cube of fish **Brand:** oz	2 cubes of combo veg: 1 cube of turkey **Brand:** oz
Details	Time: Initials:	Time: Initials:	Time: Initials:	Time: Initials:	Time: Initials:
TEA	Milk Only **Brand:** oz	Milk Only **Brand:** oz	Milk Only **Brand:** oz	Milk Only **Brand:** oz	Milk Only **Brand:** oz
Details	Time: Initials:	Time: Initials:	Time: Initials:	Time: Initials:	Time: Initials:

WEEK 8 - Weaning Programme

Age at Now: _____

	Monday	Tuesday	Wednesday	Thursday	Friday
BREAKFAST	Porridge with apple Brand: oz	Rusk Brand: oz	Porridge with pear Brand: oz	Rusk Brand: oz	Porridge with plum Brand: oz
Details	Time: Initials:	Time: Initials:	Time: Initials:	Time: Initials:	Time: Initials:
BRUNCH	Milk Only Brand: oz	Milk Only Brand: oz	Milk Only Brand: oz	Milk Only Brand: oz	Milk Only Brand: oz
Details	Time: Initials:	Time: Initials:	Time: Initials:	Time: Initials:	Time: Initials:
LUNCH	3 cubes of combo veg Brand: oz	2 cubes of combo veg: 1 cube of fish Brand: oz	3 cubes of combo veg Brand: oz	2 cubes of combo veg: 1 cube of fish Brand: oz	3 cubes of combo veg Brand: oz
Details	Time: Initials:	Time: Initials:	Time: Initials:	Time: Initials:	Time: Initials:
TEA	1 cube of combo & lentils Brand: oz	Milk Only Brand: oz	1 cube of combo & lentils Brand: oz	Milk Only Brand: oz	1 cube of combo & lentils Brand: oz
Details	Time: Initials:	Time: Initials:	Time: Initials:	Time: Initials:	Time: Initials:

WEEK 9 - Weaning Programme

Age at Now: _____

	Monday	Tuesday	Wednesday	Thursday	Friday
BREAKFAST	with fruit oz Brand:	with fruit oz Brand:	with fruit oz Brand:	with fruit oz Brand:	with fruit oz Brand:
Details	Time: Initials:	Time: Initials:	Time: Initials:	Time: Initials:	Time: Initials:
BRUNCH	Milk Only oz Brand:	Milk Only oz Brand:	Milk Only oz Brand:	Milk Only oz Brand:	Milk Only oz Brand:
Details	Time: Initials:	Time: Initials:	Time: Initials:	Time: Initials:	Time: Initials:
LUNCH	2 cubes of combo veg & 1 cube of beef Brand: oz	3 cubes of combo veg Brand: oz	2 cubes of combo veg & 1 cube of beef Brand: oz	3 cubes of combo veg Brand: oz	2 cubes of combo veg & 1 cube of turkey Brand: oz
Details	Time: Initials:	Time: Initials:	Time: Initials:	Time: Initials:	Time: Initials:
TEA	1 cube of combo: F-Food: Brand: oz	1 cube of combo: F-Food: Brand: oz	1 cube of combo: F-Food: Brand: oz	1 cube of combo: F-Food: Brand: oz	1 cube of combo: F-Food: Brand: oz
Details	Time: Initials:	Time: Initials:	Time: Initials:	Time: Initials:	Time: Initials:

WEEK 10 - Weaning Programme
Finger Foods to be introduced – please give clear details of foods given

Age at Now: _____

	Monday	Tuesday	Wednesday	Thursday	Friday
BREAKFAST Porridge/rusk with fruit	**Brand:** oz	**Brand:** oz	**Brand:** oz	**Brand:** oz	**Brand:** oz
Details	Time: Initials:	Time: Initials:	Time: Initials:	Time: Initials:	Time: Initials:
BRUNCH	Milk Only **Brand:** oz	Milk Only **Brand:** oz	Milk Only **Brand:** oz	Milk Only **Brand:** oz	Milk Only **Brand:** oz
Details	Time: Initials:	Time: Initials:	Time: Initials:	Time: Initials:	Time: Initials:
LUNCH 3-4 cubes	**Brand:** oz	**Brand:** oz	**Brand:** oz	**Brand:** oz	**Brand:** oz
Details	Time: Initials:	Time: Initials:	Time: Initials:	Time: Initials:	Time: Initials:
TEA 2-3 cubes	F-Food: **Brand:** oz	F-Food: **Brand:** oz	F-Food: **Brand:** oz	F-Food: **Brand:** oz	F-Food: **Brand:** oz
Details	Time: Initials:	Time: Initials:	Time: Initials:	Time: Initials:	Time: Initials:

WEEK 11 - Weaning Programme

Age at Now: _____

	Monday	Tuesday	Wednesday	Thursday	Friday
BREAKFAST	Porridge & pear	Rusk	Porridge & pear	Rusk	Porridge & apple
	Brand: oz	Brand: oz	Brand: oz	Brand: oz	Brand: oz
Details	Time: Initials:	Time: Initials:	Time: Initials:	Time: Initials:	Time: Initials:
BRUNCH	Milk Only	Milk Only	Milk Only	Milk Only	Milk Only
	Brand: oz	Brand: oz	Brand: oz	Brand: oz	Brand: oz
Details	Time: Initials:	Time: Initials:	Time: Initials:	Time: Initials:	Time: Initials:
LUNCH	2 cubes of combo & fish	2 cubes of combo & turkey	2 cubes of combo & fish	2 cubes of combo & turkey	2 cubes of combo & fish
	Brand: oz	Brand: oz	Brand: oz	Brand: oz	Brand: oz
Details	Time: Initials:	Time: Initials:	Time: Initials:	Time: Initials:	Time: Initials:
TEA	2 cubes of combo	2 cubes of combo	2 cubes of combo	2 cubes of combo	2 cubes of combo
	Brand: oz	Brand: oz	Brand: oz	Brand: oz	Brand: oz
Details	Time: Initials:	Time: Initials:	Time: Initials:	Time: Initials:	Time: Initials:

Weaning Programme

Age at Now: _____

	Monday	Tuesday	Wednesday	Thursday	Friday
BREAKFAST	**Brand:** **oz**	**Brand:** **oz**	**Brand:** **oz**	**Brand:** **oz**	**Brand:** **oz**
Details	Time: Initials:	Time: Initials:	Time: Initials:	Time: Initials:	Time: Initials:
BRUNCH	**Brand:** **oz**	**Brand:** **oz**	**Brand:** **oz**	**Brand:** **oz**	**Brand:** **oz**
Details	Time: Initials:	Time: Initials:	Time: Initials:	Time: Initials:	Time: Initials:
LUNCH	**Brand:** **oz**	**Brand:** **oz**	**Brand:** **oz**	**Brand:** **oz**	**Brand:** **oz**
Details	Time: Initials:	Time: Initials:	Time: Initials:	Time: Initials:	Time: Initials:
TEA	**Brand:** **oz**	**Brand:** **oz**	**Brand:** **oz**	**Brand:** **oz**	**Brand:** **oz**
Details	Time: Initials:	Time: Initials:	Time: Initials:	Time: Initials:	Time: Initials:

The aim of the Babyopathy Weaning Programme is to support your baby in their exploration of foods and textures that are beneficial to their health and development. The weaning chart shows the foods that are introduced at specific ages; at our nurseries we do not give babies foods until the age shown on the chart as these are foods that we have identified as potential allergens if introduced too early. Our weaning stages are:

STAGE 1 – *Mush four to six months*
All our first weaning cubes are prepared from fresh vegetables, puréed and frozen in ice cube size portions. The first food is always sweet potato followed by carrots, cauliflower, peas and broccoli.

These foods are introduced at lunchtime, one cube at a time, so that sleep routines are not affected at night.

Puréed fruits are only used as an accompaniment to baby rice, rusks or porridge which we introduce at breakfast at approximately six and a half months old, due to their sugar content.

STAGE 2 – *Mash six to eight months*
During this stage of weaning we introduce an additional meal at teatime which will include foods such as pulses and vegetables such as courgette.

Lunch will now have an introduction of meats and fish with turkey and white fish introduced first followed by chicken, beef and lamb. Meats will be minced but vegetables will be mashed to encourage facial muscles.

In addition, first finger foods are introduced at breakfast and teatime with foods such as steamed carrot and sweet potato, banana and rusk, chicken or fish pieces and cucumber sticks.

We still avoid citrus fruits, strawberries, potato at this stage as well as gluten, eggs and dairy.

STAGE 3 – *Munch eight to twelve months*
Here comes the really exciting stage as babies can now have the full baby menus which are now chopped into small pieces. Our baby menus use all of the foods that are shown as appropriate for the age group on the weaning chart.

Foods to avoid before one year:

I avoid these foods during the first year as if your baby is likely to develop an allergy, all of these foods have either been identified as potential allergens or as harmful to them:

Nuts ✿ **Citrus fruits** ✿ **Strawberries** ✿ **Dairy** ✿ **Honey**
Eggs ✿ **Gluten** ✿ **Shellfish** ✿ **Chocolate** ✿ **Salt**

One of the most important foods to avoid for all babies and children is salt. Salt, or sodium, is naturally occurring in many foods without being added during the cooking process. One of the main reasons we avoid products such as cheese, bread, yogurt and baked beans is because of their salt content. When consumed on a regular basis they can easily cause a baby or child's diet to exceed the maximum recommended salt levels.

Finally, from their first birthday they will be introduced to cow's milk and other dairy products and move on to our Nascuropathy Nutrition plans which includes gluten.

It is important that your baby's first taste should be savoury and not sweet so that their palate is steered away from the 'sweet tooth' variety. We introduce sweet potato first because it has a pleasant sweeter taste of all the savoury vegetables but it is also high in vitamin C with a good iron content, so this means that you are already contributing to your baby's iron supply.

Now I must stress that at the start of weaning you are purely introducing tastes and textures which is why we only use one standard ice cube size for a portion. Even with this small amount it is an introduction and not a requirement that they eat it all or that it is seen as a substitute for milk consumption.

Nursery Baby Menus

Morning (am session)   Breakfast (20% EAR- 240kcal)   8.15 – 8.45 am   &   Brunch (10% of EAR-120kcal)   10.45 – 11.15am

WEEK 1	Monday	Tuesday	Wednesday	Thursday	Friday
Breakfast	Hot Oat Cereal Porridge (made with formula) with dried fruit	Gluten free toasted fingers with spread & dried fruit	Rice Snaps with formula milk Gluten free tea cake & spread	Gluten free toasted fingers with spread & fruit salad	Yogurt & fruit salad **No citrus**
Allergy Angels					
Brunch	Rice cakes with cheese spread and apple	Yogurt & pear	Gluten free muffins and spread with fruit **No citrus**	Yogurt with "phenomenal rainbow" fruit **No citrus**	Gluten free breadsticks with cheese and cucumber
Allergy Angels					
Lunch	Rice Spaghetti Bolognese with "extraordinary orange" sauce **No tomato/pepper**	Fish Without Fingers with "white wonder" mash, peas & sweetcorn **No potato**	Roast Turkey with "remarkable rainbow" vegetable wedges **No pepper**	Lamb Curry with "marvellous yellow" sauce **No tomato/pepper**	Salmon Rice Pasta with "white wonder & extraordinary orange" sauces **No tomato**
Allergy Angels					
High-Tea	Gluten free wrap with crunchy vegetables & cheese **No tomato/pepper**	Gluten free toasted fingers with spread and carrot and cucumber sticks	Cheese & gluten free crackers with celery & pineapple	Gluten free Pitta Bread with Tuna dip & crudités **No pepper**	Rice cakes with cream cheese & berries
Allergy Angels					

(Supper is recommended at home between 6.30 – 7.30pm)

Food Group	Examples	Recommended Servings
Starchy Foods (gluten free)	Bread, pasta, noodles, rice, other grains, cereals, sweet potato	4 per day
Meat, Fish & Proteins	Meat, poultry, fish, meat alternatives, pulses	2 per day

Food Group	Examples	Recommended Servings
Fruit & Veg	Fresh, frozen, canned, dried and juiced fruit and vegetables and pulses	5 per day
Milk & Dairy	Milk, cheese, yogurt, fromage frais	3 per day

209

Nursery Baby Menus

Morning (am session) Breakfast (20% EAR- 240kcal) 8.15 – 8.45 am & Brunch (10% of EAR-120kcal) 10.45 – 11.15am

WEEK 2	Monday	Tuesday	Wednesday	Thursday	Friday
Breakfast	Gluten free toasted fingers with spread & dried fruit	Gluten free toasted fingers with spread & banana	Hot Oat Cereal Porridge (with formula milk) & berries	Yogurt & raisins	Rice snaps with formula milk Gluten free tea cake & spread
Allergy Angels					
Brunch	Gluten free crumpet with spread and cucumber and berries	Gluten free muffin with spread and melon	Rice cakes with cream cheese and apple	Gluten free toasted tea cakes with spread	Cheese and gluten free crackers with berries and cucumber
Allergy Angels					
Lunch	Chinese Chicken with "white wonder & extraordinary orange" sauces and rice **No tomato**	Mixed bean and root vegetable stew with "extraordinary orange" sauce and apricot cous cous **No pepper**	Gluten free pizza of the day with "extraordinary orange" sauce and green beans	Salmon & Broccoli Lasagne (gluten free) with "extraordinary orange & white wonder" sauces	Beef chilli with "extraordinary orange and perfect purple" sauces & rice
Allergy Angels					
High-Tea	Rice cakes with fruit salad **No citrus**	Gluten free pitta bread with hummus and crudités **No pepper**	Yogurt with fruit salad and granola topping **No citrus**	Gluten free crumpet with cream cheese and berries and pineapple	Gluten free toasted bagel with tuna dip and mange tout
Allergy Angels					

(Supper is recommended at home between 6.30 – 7.30pm)

Food Group	Examples	Recommended Servings
Starchy Foods (gluten free)	Bread, pasta, noodles, rice, other grains, cereals, sweet potato	4 per day
Meat, Fish & Proteins	Meat, poultry, fish, meat alternatives, pulses	2 per day

Food Group	Examples	Recommended Servings
Fruit & Veg	Fresh, frozen, canned, dried and juiced fruit and vegetables and pulses	5 per day
Milk & Dairy	Milk, cheese, yogurt, fromage frais	3 per day

Organic or not organic

That is the question. Well this debate has been going on for years. If you read some organic books they tell you everything should be organic. However, I believe this is a complete waste of money. There are some products that if I had a choice I would recommend be organic but not everything needs to be (I think I covered this in the Before Travelling section).

Once your baby has reached 12 months and moves on to cow's milk then for me it should be organic; if you can also buy organic fruit and vegetables then that is a bonus too. But again, if you can't don't feel guilty, just buying and cooking fresh fruits and vegetables is a step in the right direction.

Avoiding allergies

Allergies seem to be becoming an increasing issue in the world today. Whether this is due to more sensitive testing or the increased use of genetically modified foods and 'added artificial ingredients' we cannot tell. However, it is important that if an allergy is highlighted it is managed appropriately.

My first step towards managing allergies is to use the weaning plan I have given you in this book which through introducing specific foods at specific times and withholding others works towards reducing asthma, eczema and allergies. By being aware through the initial weaning phase of when to introduce certain foods can have a dramatic effect on the development of allergies.

Even with this some children still develop allergies because of their own genetics and it is important to manage this effectively. For nurseries I developed an allergy management system, which you can use at home too, based around a colour-coded system for the main allergens as follows:

One of the best ways to ensure your baby avoids developing an allergy is to follow the specific introduction of foods during weaning according to our weaning chart as it avoids all of the potential allergens until your baby is of an age to handle them.

Commercial baby food

I feel at this time a little attention is needed on the subject of commercial baby food. There are many varieties of baby food on the market today and until recently all of these were presented either dried in a packet or ready to serve in a long shelf life jar.

Only recently I watched a TV programme investigating fad diets and the reporter tried the 'baby food diet' and described it as a mess of puréed food that has been regurgitated and put in a jar to eat again. Have you ever tried some of these foods? Really appealing aren't they? I wouldn't want to eat it every day yet we give it to our babies.

I remember walking down the baby food aisle in Tesco and seeing a man standing staring at the shelves. He had a young baby in the trolley that I am guessing was about four months old. There was a multitude of baby food in front of him and he had obviously been sent out to get weaning food for his young baby. His only guide was the age label on the jar. What shocked me though was his eventual choice was a tray of chocolate pudding 'from four months old'.

Why do commercial baby food companies even make these products? Babies do not need desserts, they certainly do not need the sugar-filled varieties in their weaning plan. So why make them?

My other concern is some of the newer brands that because they are 'organic' parents instantly assume they are better and healthier for their babies.

I went to lunch with a friend whose daughter was seven months and weaning. Her mum pulled out a pouch of fruit purée, 'Look, it's organic,' she said with a big smile on her face. She squeezed it into a bowl and gave the baby a spoonful; well, the little one pulled such a face which I jokingly call 'pouch face'. I looked at the packet and there was the equivalent of two teaspoons of sugar in it. Mum tasted it and pulled an even worse face!

Whilst I do not want to put anyone out of business, I implore you to think twice about commercial baby food and if you do use it look closely at the labelling. Use it as a backup or as an emergency meal but do your best not to use it as their entire source of food.

If you can prepare your own using fresh fruits and vegetables (herbs and spices later too) then that is what is ultimately best for your baby and I think even the large baby food manufacturers would have a hard time arguing that one!

Finger foods

It used to be that as soon as you started to wean your baby you would give them a spoon to hold. This not only encouraged their grip reflex but also their hand-eye coordination as they attempted to get that spoon into their mouth.

As weaning started earlier when my children were young, by the time they reached six months old they had mastered the art of getting what they were holding into their mouth and so knew exactly what to do with that first carrot stick as soon as you handed it over!

Of course, because they had already been through the first purée stage of weaning and were now on to the lumpy mashed stage, chewing on a piece of parboiled carrot was no problem at all. Nowadays because weaning doesn't even begin until six months, finger foods are being introduced later and we are seeing additional developmental delays in motor skills and of course speech as I have already mentioned.

Finger foods are essential as some of the crucial skills are learnt and developed with finger foods:

- ❀ *Hand-eye coordination*
- ❀ *Manual dexterity*
- ❀ *Language*

However, if your baby has only just been introduced to puréed food then do not give finger foods. Once they have mastered the art of having food in their mouth and therefore have developed their mouth muscles and chewing action then you can introduce finger foods.

Food Introduction Chart

Food Product	0-5 mths milk only	5-6 mths mush	6-8 mths mash	8-12 mths munch	12+mths Full Menu
Milk & Dairy	FF – Finger Food Introduction				
Breast/Formula Milk	X	X	X	X	X
Cheese/Yogurt/Butter/Spread				X	X
Cow's Milk				X	X
Eggs					
Eggs/Powdered Egg					X
Wheat Products					
Bread					X
Pasta					X
Cereals - wheat based incl. Barley					X
Fish					
White Fish (no bones)		X	X	X	X
Oily Fish (no bones)				X	X
Small boned fish					X
Fruits					
Apple/Pear/Banana/Plum		X	FF	X	X
Melon/Mango/Apricot			X	X	X
Grapes/Berries				X	X
Citrus/Strawberries				X	X
Tomato/Pepper					X
Nuts					
Nuts					X
Products containing nuts					X
Vegetables/Salad					
Sweet Potato/Carrot/Swede		X	FF	X	X
Cauliflower/Broccoli/Peas		X	FF	X	X
Green Beans/Courgettes etc		X	FF	X	X
Lettuce/Cucumber		X	FF	X	X
Meat/Protein					
Pulses/Lentils		X	X	X	X
Beef/Lamb			X	X	X
Turkey/Chicken			FF	X	X
Other Foods					
Baby Rice/Porridge, Rusk		X	X	X	X
Rice			X	X	X
Potato			X	X	X
Oats			X	X	X

Cutlery, cups and etiquette!

When you start to wean, give your baby a spoon to hold, at first it just keeps their hands occupied but eventually they will copy your actions and try to feed themselves. They gradually get more and more into their mouths until you don't have to feed them anymore!

Once your baby has started to wean you can introduce a lidded cup so that they get used to drinking from something other than a bottle or breast. I have always found the free-flow ones best and just help your baby rather than the ones they have to suck hard to get anything from. You want your baby to want to drink from it and get plenty of water not turn it into an Olympic event!

Finally, a little about etiquette. Again, babies are a blank canvas and learn by observing and copying, so even at this young age make mealtimes the way they should be, about eating and connecting as a family. It is not play time, and certainly not TV/screen time! Teaching them from the beginning that it is about eating together, talking to them and only when finished can they get down and play time begins again will give them important skills for life.

One year on

Once your baby gets to a year old they can pretty much have everything except nuts, these should be avoided until five years old according to current guidelines.

It is very important that your baby is eating their minimum five a day of fruits and vegetables (with an emphasis on vegetables) and at the nurseries I have developed a range of what we call Super Sauces that each contain both a source of protein as well as two or three fruits or vegetables. As the main focus of the weaning and nutrition plan is to ensure the children eat a complete rainbow of foods a day it made sense to create a rainbow of sauces too!

These can then be added into the children's main meal of the day and quite often we will add two of these sauces ensuring the children in our care are eating a super vitamin and mineral boosting meal. These sauces are great for all the family especially if you have fussy children (or husbands like I had) and one or two of them contain a great source of folate too which is an essential vitamin for pregnant mums especially in the first trimester. So get cooking and freeze meal-size portions in all the rainbow colours so you can add them to your meals too.

My Super Sauces

You can use these sauces individually in meals or you can pair them up to give an extra boost to your meals. The only one I feel works perfectly on its own is the White Wonder.

Super Red

Ingredients: *1 can chopped tomatoes (or 5 fresh with the skin removed) ½ red onion, 150g raspberries, ½ can adzuki beans, 150ml vegetable stock or water if have allergies, 1 tsp olive oil*

Lightly sweat the red onion in the olive oil in a saucepan until soft and translucent. Add the remaining ingredients and simmer for approximately 30 minutes or until beans are soft. Blitz with a blender to a smooth consistency and put into individual containers or food bags to freeze until needed.

Good source of protein

Great source of lycopene to boost brain function and digestion and is therefore great for whichever end of the age scale you may be (grandparents included)

Contains zinc to promote a healthy immune system

Contains vitamin C, beta carotene and iron so great for fighting viruses

Super in meals such as spaghetti bolognese, in the meat part of your lasagne, on your pizza base, beef casserole and even put a little in beef burgers.

Marvellous Yellow

*Ingredients: 1 medium swede chopped,
1 can of chickpeas, 1 leek, juice of ½ a lemon,
150ml vegetable stock, 1 tsp olive oil*

Lightly sweat the leek in the olive oil in a saucepan until soft
and translucent. Add the remaining ingredients and simmer
for approximately 30 minutes or until chickpeas and swede are
soft. Blitz with a blender to a smooth consistency and put into
individual containers or food bags to freeze until needed.

Good source of protein

*Contains iron, vitamin B6 and calcium to promote
a healthy immune system, bones and blood*

Contains vitamin C for fighting off viruses

Marvellous in meals such as chicken casserole,
fish pie, lamb tagine and even a chicken curry.

Extraordinary Orange

Ingredients: 1 butternut squash chopped, 1 sweet potato chopped, 250g red lentils, ½ onion, 2 apricots, 150ml vegetable stock, 1 tsp olive oil

Lightly sweat the onion in the olive oil in a saucepan until soft and translucent. Add the remaining ingredients and simmer for approximately 30 minutes or until all ingredients are soft. Blitz with a blender to a smooth consistency and put into individual containers or food bags to freeze until needed.

Good source of protein

Great source of antioxidants to fight off colds and flu bugs

*Contains iron, zinc and calcium to promote
a healthy immune system, bones and blood*

Contains carotenoids to promote healthy cell growth

Extraordinary in meals such as cannelloni and pasta bake.

Perfect Purple

Ingredients: 1 aubergine, 1 can red kidney beans,
½ red onion, 1 red pepper 150g blackberries,
150ml vegetable stock, 1 tsp olive oil

Lightly sweat the red onion in the olive oil in a saucepan until soft and translucent. Add the remaining ingredients and simmer for approximately 30 minutes or until beans are soft. Blitz with a blender to a smooth consistency and put into individual containers or food bags to freeze until needed.

Good source of protein

Great source of antioxidants and vitamin C
to fight off colds and flu bugs

Contains vitamin E to help boost the immune system

Contains folate which helps promote brain stem function
and is great in the first trimester of pregnancy

Perfect in meals such as chilli con carne, ratatouille
and three bean stew.

White Wonder

*Ingredients: ½ (500g approx.) cauliflower,
1 can cannellini beans, 1 leek,
150ml vegetable stock, 1 tsp olive oil*

Lightly sweat the leek in the olive oil in a saucepan until soft and translucent. Add the remaining ingredients and simmer for approximately 30 minutes or until beans are soft. Blitz with a blender to a smooth consistency and put into individual containers or food bags to freeze until needed.

Good source of protein

Great source of calcium and iron for healthy bones and beautiful blood

Promotes a healthy immune system

Contains folate which helps promote brain stem function and is great in the first trimester of pregnancy

Wonderful as a secret boost to mashed potato, the white sauce in your lasagne or in a cheese sauce based dish!

If using vegetable stock then look for one that doesn't contain gluten or if not available just use water for babies under one year or if anyone has allergies.

All of the recipes should make approximately one litre of sauce, which I suggest you split into four portions. With the exception of the White Wonder Sauce, which I use on its own particularly in mashed potatoes, I try to use two different portions of sauce in each main meal giving the approximate equivalent of three of the recommended five a day.

Combinations that I think go well are:

✓ *Super Red and Extraordinary Orange*

✓ *Marvellous Yellow and Perfect Purple*

✓ *Super Red and Perfect Purple*

Don't forget that for dishes that may have a meat element as well as a pasta or potato element you can use either a Super Red or Perfect Purple in your meat and a White Wonder in your pasta white sauce or mashed potatoes too. It makes a lasagne or shepherd's pie packed with extra special vitamins and minerals and no one will ever know!

Old-fashioned values

I thought I would end this section by talking a little about old-fashioned values as they have been a guiding light for me throughout my life and my business.

Manners

Manners cost nothing, it's something my grandmother used to say to me for as long as I can remember and it is a phrase I have always continued to use. My grandmother was responsible for my name and ultimately the name of my first nursery as she used to call me her 'little angel' and it seemed fitting that this was the name I gave my nursery. Unfortunately, it wasn't a unique name and that was something I decided we needed when we introduced my programme into the nurseries and so Angels at Play was born.

After 25 years owning my nurseries I decided it was time for me to sell them and retire from the world of day care and focus on my passion: bringing Babyopathy to every mum and baby that wants it.

However, my grandmother's values always stayed with me and are something I like to see continued in the nurseries. Please and thank you, as she said, cost nothing and is very easy to teach to your baby if they are second nature to you. It goes back to my ethos of constant interaction; if you use please and thank you, even when interacting with your baby, then they will soon copy you.

However, manners aren't just please and thank you. I have mentioned etiquette before and I fear it is a dying art, but it doesn't have to be.

I think it is important that families should be able to go out to dinner or to the theatre or wherever they so wish, but so often when I am in a restaurant etc. I see families allowing their children to throw food, sit and scream or even worse, run around. I want to ask every parent, 'When did this become good manners and acceptable?'

Respect, boundaries and older children

I am afraid I may well have another soap box moment here!

Once again, I refer to my grandmother who used to say, 'When we were young children were seen but not heard.' Now I am not suggesting that we need to go that far back in the raising of our children but things have definitely swung too far in the other direction.

The problem we have now since the ban on smacking is there are no boundaries whatsoever. My children had boundaries, they had rules and manners and I didn't need to use force or scream at them, as I now hear so many parents doing. So many children I see today don't have boundaries, they 'run rings' around their parents, use tantrums to get what they want and parents so often give in for a quiet life or scream at them, grab their arms and whisper threats instead – is this a better way?

I would just like to say it does not give you a quiet life, it just gives the signal to your children that you have no intention of seeing through what you say.

There are so many news reports on the lack of respect from children and out of control behaviour, where do you think it starts? At home!

I know this is a 'baby' book but here's a statistic you should know:

> *The number of primary school children expelled has more than doubled over a four-year period. Meanwhile, 6,685 children at state schools in England were permanently excluded in 2015/16, up from 5,795 the year before and some as young as four years old.*

I would like to make it clear that the following statement is of course not aimed at a child that has a diagnosed medical or development condition.

No means NO

Now as stupid as it sounds I would like to point out that no means no. Not maybe or when I'm not looking or I'm talking and don't want to get up and make you stop.

There is no point in giving one, two or three strikes before you get up and stop your child from doing whatever it is you don't want them to do. All you are teaching them is that they can do it two or three times before you act.

Basically, a green light for bad behaviour and rising stress levels for you. This current trend of helicopter parenting and time-poor, guilt-ridden parents is creating a time bomb of behaviour and mental health issues as well as developmental and educational delays. All because we don't mean no when we say it and back it up with boundaries, respect and manners.

'But they're only babies,' I hear you cry!

By the time your baby is 10 months old their memory skills will have improved and recall of words and tones of voices will now have a meaning and they understand the concept of 'no'. Within weeks your baby will be even more mobile than they are now, and so beginning to introduce boundaries now and helping them understand 'no' can have a huge effect on their safety and well-being as they become fully mobile and even more inquisitive! No matter how much you baby-proof your home there are always times when you can see something about to happen and if 'no means no' you have a better chance of stopping it.

Establish rules and boundaries from the start and life is actually easier. Children actually feel more secure and develop better when given boundaries, setting boundaries shows you care and instils respect. Your child will not love you less if you set boundaries. However, you have to see it through when you say no. What kind of boundaries are we talking about?

✓ *NO MEANS NO! To be honest this is the main one!*

✓ *Teach please and thank you right from the beginning*

✓ *Have a mealtime etiquette (we have one at nursery) – most importantly mealtimes are for sitting still and eating, not running around, climbing about the furniture or watching a screen*

And as they get older so will their boundaries grow.

If boundaries are in place, when you have your second or third child, life again is easier. Whatever age your children are, when a new baby comes along they naturally have a jealous reaction to the fact they are no longer the sole centre of your attention.

Many parents tell me that they feel guilty about setting boundaries for their older children, usually two or three years old, when their new baby arrives. However, often when the tantrums start or their patience is tested by the older child acting up they end up losing their temper and shout or worse, and then guess what, feel guilty. So, you feel guilty if you put boundaries in place but even more guilty when you shout or lose your temper. Which is worse?

If you had put the boundaries in place straight away, yes, your older child will still naturally test those boundaries, but when you reinforce them you also reinforce their sense of security and well-being and save your patience and guilt in the long run.

A year already?

One year old, it is a huge milestone to be celebrated and signifies the end of 'babyhood' and here comes 'toddlerhood'. I think a first birthday party to celebrate their achievements so far is an absolute must, as is cake, but please remember they really don't need all the bells and whistles with miniature ponies and a mountain of presents – time with you and some fun and games is enough (they won't remember it anyway!).

Your baby will have achieved so much in their first year and here are as many of the milestones that I could think of:

- ❁ *Can stand alone, some taking first steps, even walking (my son was a Tasmanian devil, ooops sorry, walking and running at nine months!).*

- ❁ *Should be using a cup for water, some babies do not need to have lids but I would save that for home when it doesn't matter if you need yet another change of clothes!*

- ❁ *Can feed themselves with a spoon although how much starts on the spoon and ends up in the mouth is not yet a guaranteed thing.*

- ❁ *Has mastered the art of picking things up in each hand, is quite good at banging them together and even better at dropping them on the floor for you to pick up. If they are particularly 'sporty' they may even be throwing things by now (food seems to always be preferred over a ball for some reason!).*

- ❁ *The pincer movement is particularly refined and babies have an inbuilt ability to spot something unsuitable from 50 paces (might take them a while to get there though!) so be aware of choking hazards.*

❀ *Can understand simple commands and requests so don't be fooled, and yes they do recognise their own name even if they may pretend not to.*

❀ *Can say quite a few words, particularly likes to copy you so do be careful what you say around your one-year-old as it's never the good words they choose if there's a bad one to be copied!*

❀ *Understands the relevance of actions and can wave 'bye-bye' for example but may also put their arms up to you as they know what it means now.*

❀ *Your baby loves to point and as we've already established at this age it's not rude, nurture their inquisitive nature and tell them what it is they are pointing at.*

❀ *Your baby will start to recognise they can go 'over and under' things for example so begin to use these descriptive words when they do something.*

❀ *They can sit still for short times for you to engage them in a book or an activity.*

❀ *They will love familiar songs and rhymes and be able to imitate familiar actions and even tones and pitches in their own singing style.*

Your baby has reached the end of their Babyopathy journey but with your help is now a sensory aware, inquisitive, well-rounded toddler in the making ready for their next journey… Nascuropathy!

The Nascuropathy ethos for your toddler is, show them:

✓ *They are beautiful just the way they are and so is everyone else – no judgment and no jealousy*

✓ *They are strong and independent with boundaries of beautiful behaviour – explore, experiment and experience but no means no!*

✓ *They can be anything they want to be if they try and try again – let them see inspiration and determination*

✓ *Be compassionate to others and the world around us –* beauty is how we treat others and care for our world

✓ *Manners, respect and etiquette cost nothing but are invaluable to have* – the power of positivity can be seen through the reactions to a smile!

Children are born as a blank canvas, they become what they see, hear and feel, so there really is only you and those you let them interact with who are responsible for who they become…

The Relaxed Mum CHECKLIST

✓ **Know your baby's sensory developmental journey and how you can nurture it**

✓ **Keep screens away from babies, they don't need technology, they need you!**

✓ **Interaction with your baby is the key to nurturing their development**

✓ **Make some time for you, you are still a person and time with friends etc. will be beneficial for your mental and emotional well-being**

✓ **Spend time with your baby out in nature and help them explore**

✓ **Encourage their physical development, it is the precursor to their cognitive development**

✓ **Tummy time!**

✓ **You don't need expensive toys, use natural resources**

✓ **Every baby is unique, don't compare and don't judge**

✓ **Your baby is a blank canvas, paint it with positivity, individuality and compassion**

✓ **Sleep is key to your baby's development, sleep when they sleep if you need to**

✓ **No medals are won for doing everything! Do what you can and what's important – ironing can wait!**

✓ **Weaning is a key stage of development, it can affect their future health so know what they need**

✓ **No means no!**

✓ **Keep using your Babyopathy toolkits, they really do work!**

Chapter Eleven

Returning to Work

Relaxed Mum, Contented Baby!

Returning to Work

I have included this section as being a working mum is a reality and not a choice for many new mums now. However, I want to make it clear that whether you are a non-working mum or a working mum, being a relaxed mum means making the right choice for you and your family and not judging others for the decisions they make.

If you are returning to work, there are some important things to consider.

Leaving your baby

At some point after your baby is born there comes a time when you have to leave your baby with someone else. To some new parents this fills them with complete dread especially if they do not have close family nearby.

Your first experience of leaving your baby may be with a babysitter so you can have a couple of hours with your partner and quite often this will be a family member but sometimes you have to rely on someone not quite as close to the family.

It is always important to ensure that the person you are leaving your baby with is competent to be left. This may seem like a stupid statement to some people, why would you leave your baby with someone who wasn't competent but it has happened. The teenage child of a friend who you've known for a long time and always been a well-mannered, respectable child or the 30-something childless friend who is eager to help out. They may all be well intentioned but may not have the knowledge or experience to deal with a baby that won't stop crying or may not have the knowledge to never fall asleep on the sofa with a baby on their chest. Too many times I have read these tragic stories and sometimes it has led to the parents being prosecuted too for negligence.

My point is not to scare you into never leaving your baby as it is important for them to socialise as well as you. What is important though is to make sure the person with whom you leave your baby is competent and has up-to-date information.

How can you do this? Well one of the best things you can do is ensure they have attended a basic paediatric first aid course. They are not expensive and only a couple of hours long, but even for grandparents can be an eye opener when it comes to handling emergency situations or just being more aware.

Secondly, if they are not a family member you can request they have a DBS check completed (Disclosure & Barring Service). It is a certificate that all childcare professionals have to have and is re-checked whenever they move to a new employer. It is a little bit of effort and cost for huge peace of mind.

Leaving your baby at a nursery or childminder though is a completely different scenario. This is not just for an odd hour but potentially for long days and for some five days a week.

It was important for me, when parents viewed my nurseries, that they too felt like they were entering a sensory oasis, and felt just as relaxed and welcome as their babies!

When you walk into a nursery, yes it is important it is clean and safe and welcoming but more importantly it is the staff you need to feel comfortable with. They need to be friendly and knowledgeable, professional and aware of their surroundings. They need to instil confidence and you need to be comfortable in your choices.

What is important in any situation is that you have prepared both yourself and your baby in advance. You would be surprised at the number of parents we have had turn up with their babies on their first day at nursery with a bottle in hand saying, 'I have only breastfed up til now.' What a traumatic day that is for all concerned, staff included! If you're breastfeeding and returning to work, wean your baby on to bottles well in advance of being left.

Think about your baby's routine and how it will be affected by your journey to nursery/childminder and home again. The last thing you need when driving home is a baby crying because they are too tired or too hungry.

It is surprising how many new parents think about their return to work and everything they need to do but do not realise the implications it may have on their baby's routine or breastfeeding etc.

Separation anxiety

Whenever you leave your baby, especially for the first time, you will feel separation anxiety, but you are an adult and can understand why you're leaving and that you will be coming back. Your baby doesn't. At first, a baby doesn't realise they are an individual, why would they, they have spent the last nine months being part of you and you are all they need when they are first born. It is only at about six to seven months old that they will begin to realise that they are independent to you and may cry when you leave them even for a minute.

At nursery, we saw a huge change in how babies settled at nursery when the maternity rules changed. When we first opened 20 years ago, most babies started at 12 weeks old when SMP finished and by the time they reached six to seven months old their separation anxiety was less because they already had a bond with their carers.

However, in more recent years because parents now delay their nursery start to when their baby is typically six to nine months old due to the new maternity rules, separation anxiety is quite often another major hurdle both parents and babies are having to deal with during their first weeks at nursery. This also has an impact on the staff and other children at nursery too, something that isn't often acknowledged.

My recommendation to any parent that will be using a nursery when they return to work, if you can, start your baby earlier so they can bond with their new environment and the people who will be caring for them, so when they do naturally go through separation anxiety, they already have familiar faces to reassure them.

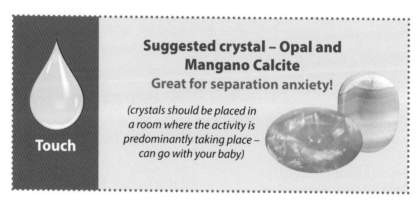

Touch

Suggested crystal – Opal and Mangano Calcite
Great for separation anxiety!

(crystals should be placed in a room where the activity is predominantly taking place – can go with your baby)

The Relaxed Mum CHECKLIST

✓ **Be happy in your decision, even if you feel you had no choice; it will make a difference to your own and your baby's mental well-being**

✓ **Plan ahead – it is better to make informed choices than rushed ones**

✓ **If you visit a nursery when you're pregnant make sure you visit again with your baby so you can see how the staff interact and how comfortable you are with your choice**

✓ **Seven to nine months is key for separation anxiety development – avoid starting nursery during this time, if possible start before**

Chapter Twelve
Dad's Army - Dads Matter Too!

Relaxed Mum, Contented Baby!

Dad's Army - Dads Matter Too!

Let me say first that I appreciate not everyone will have the baby's dad present in their lives for whatever reason, and whilst the 'romantic' role can be fulfilled by a 'significant other', for those that are single by choice or by circumstance please feel free to jump past this bit. However, there are some roles that a good friend can fulfil so some of my ramblings may be relevant. To make my life easier when writing (I hope you forgive me) I shall write as if I'm talking in this section to the dads!

So, you're going to be a dad! How do you feel?

Most dads I speak to tend to say that no one ever asks them how they feel or if they are prepared or even if they are scared, and believe me it's OK to be scared. Roles have changed a lot over the years and long gone are the days when dads sat outside in the waiting room whilst mum gave birth, and baby was raised by mum with an occasional interaction from dad.

Now, dads are expected to be by mum's side throughout the entire birth, attend all the classes, join in the feeding and know just as much as mum. Oh, and still go to work.

Now for some, being a new dad can bring some new symptoms:

- ❀ *Backache*
- ❀ *Constant tiredness*
- ❀ *Irritability*

As the husband of one of my Babyopathy consultants (you know who you are Kevin Budd – don't worry, his wife gave me permission to name him!) found out, these minor symptoms were given the name 'daddyitis' by his doctor due to the hours new dads may spend at a kitchen sink washing and sterilising baby bottles or bending over a cot or changing a nappy, all putting new variations of strain on dad's back and you have the cause of another symptom of 'daddyitis'

Now, I do not want you to think I am being flippant, quite the contrary, I think it is very much an issue that is often ignored or even 'swept under the carpet' because of male pride, but it is important and does need to be addressed and feedback from our dads' groups is that the name 'daddyitis' allows them to talk about it or initiate a conversation with friends without feeling pressured or the stigma of the 'post-natal depression' label.

It is extremely important that if you feel you may be suffering from these symptoms, or the more serious ones below, that you speak to your GP because during the first weeks of your baby's life, your partner will be relying on you quite heavily:

- ❀ *Mood swings*
- ❀ *Stress*
- ❀ *Feeling worthless*
- ❀ *Resentment towards your partner or the baby*

Post-natal depression in dads is not as widely acknowledged, but due to the change in roles over the years, the added financial pressures faced by families when mum goes on maternity leave and also the pressures of bringing up a baby in today's judgmental world amongst other things, means it is increasing and needs to be talked about.

Dad's role

One of the most important roles you can fulfil is to support your partner in their first few weeks – emotionally, physically and spiritually.

All of the symptoms I listed previously for 'daddyitis' are signs you should look for in your partner too as in the first few weeks after giving birth around 85% of new mothers can suffer from the 'baby blues'. Whilst this is considered normal and most mums rebound to feeling a little more in control around eight to 12 weeks after the birth, around 10-15% can develop much more serious symptoms of post-natal depression (PND) and will need to see their GP.

Lack of sleep can be one of the major contributors to PND and so working together to find a routine whereby you both get some sleep as soon as possible is really important for the sanity of the entire household!

If your partner is breastfeeding then this may not be easy to do as very obviously you cannot take turns with feeding, but you can at least take over nappy and bathing duties to enable even an extra hour or two of sleep for your partner.

If however your baby is bottle fed (or you have introduced a bottle to your baby once breastfeeding is established) then there is an ideal opportunity to take over a feed so that your partner can get at least a few hours of unbroken sleep. I have always found that the best feed for dad to take responsibility for is the late night 9-11pm feed (or thereabouts). Mum can get some sleep after the early evening feed and be refreshed enough to cope with the overnight feeds and dad can then get enough sleep to get up and go to work the next day.

More importantly this is an ideal time for a little daddy and baby bonding time!

Bonding with your baby

Everyone talks about the bond that mum has with the baby; however, it is just as important for dad to bond with baby too. It can be quite difficult for dad to bond during the first few weeks of baby's life, especially if mum is breastfeeding, and dad can be left overwhelmed with the whole encompassing way a baby can take over your lives.

The best way is to begin that bond when baby is in the womb:

- ✿ *Give baby a nickname once you have their first scan picture*
- ✿ *Join mum in a daily meditation, I suggest the 'Connection' meditation and place your hands on her belly too*
- ✿ *Take turns to read to baby in the womb at what will be their bedtime*
- ✿ *Make a playlist of favourite music and play it to mum and baby throughout the pregnancy and during labour*
- ✿ *Take a basic heka balancing course and you can give heka to mum and baby*
- ✿ *Learn about the Babyopathy toolkits too so you can be a part of their journey*

It is also quite common for dads to not know how to interact and bond with their baby; my best advice, don't try too hard. The easiest thing to do is cuddle your baby and when you do, talk to them. They won't understand what you are saying at first so anything will do, even what you have done that day, they will just recognise and find comfort in your pitches and tones. As the weeks go past and your baby begins to focus on your facial features just smile away and continue talking. The rest you will find will come naturally.

Touch

Suggested crystal – Blue Chalcedony
To encourage bonding
with baby
(crystals should be placed in a room where the activity is predominantly taking place or can be worn by dad)

What about me?

One of the biggest adjustments for new dads is not the amount of sleep they will get but the realisation that they are no longer the most important person in their partner's world!

Mums, generally, have an instant bond with their baby that has been building during their entire pregnancy and culminating in the effort and pain of a birth and holding the little miracle in her arms.

For dads, their world didn't really change much during pregnancy except for maybe having to tie shoelaces in the last few weeks and ensuring mum's food cravings were catered for. Then, one day their world is turned upside down, they have to watch their partner endure unimaginable pain (and I'm sorry dads but you will **never** experience pain like childbirth unless strapped to a simulation machine I once saw demonstrated on TV!) and for some this is a shock on its own, but then there is the birth! My children's father decided he wanted to photograph the birth of our daughter and I heard a range of comments over the few days following her birth from 'I'm so glad I only saw that through a camera lens' to 'I can only compare the after-effects to a baboon's bottom' – nice! But in truth, that's how much he was shocked.

If you take anything away from reading this, expect the unexpected, your life won't ever be the same, and 'don't panic Mr Mainwaring!' (Did you get the Dad's Army reference there?)

When talking to mums though, what they quite often feel is that they are neglecting their partner and if they felt they weren't being so selfish many dads would definitely be saying, 'What about me?'

Dad now isn't the most important person in the world to their partner and they have to accept this and adjust. In addition, a physical relationship stops overnight and, for some, doesn't resume for quite some time. This is probably the hardest aspect for dads to deal with.

It is important for both of you to maintain some kind of physical bond. I am not talking full-blown sex and role play (if you have the energy for that I'm impressed) but what is imperative is the contact that just reassures both of you that:

✿ *You are loved*

✿ *You are wanted*

✿ *You are still attractive*

…but, you just don't quite have the energy or the time right now.

Just by making time each day for a cuddle when you both manage to be in the bed at the same time, or to be honest any time of day, helps to keep that emotional bond between you until you are both ready to take the physical step again.

Interactive dads

I thought I would finish this section for dads with a little bit about interaction. I was shocked at a recent news article that said parents and particularly dads do not know how to interact with their babies. The article did not really give any explanation for this – but dads, don't despair. It's not rocket science, there is no right or wrong and there certainly aren't any boundaries when it comes to 'my baby is a girl, I only know boy things'.

When your baby is born, boy or girl, they won't have a clue what they are. All they want is to feel safe, secure and fed! Even if your partner is breastfeeding you can take part in everything else. In fact, breastfeeding is the only part of this book that doesn't really apply to dads – you can do everything else too.

So, all you have to do is remember the sensory approach and you're well on the way. Talk to your baby, use facial expressions, sing, play finger games, and lie on the floor, you're just as important in their lives too!

Our workshop for dads is called **Dad's Army,** a pun from the old TV programme as, let's face it, it will either be a military operation or a comedy affair; watching my son pee in my then husband's face as he tried to do his nappy was a classic episode! So, as well as all of the advice above I also put together a little toolkit for dads, they need to take care of themselves too!

Dad's Army - Babyopathy Toolkit

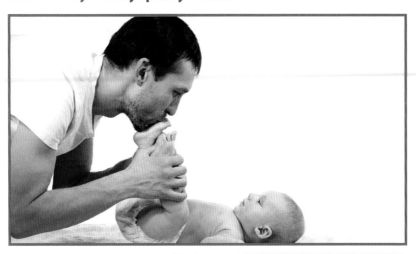

Oils

Our Routine in the Womb Blend

is not just for mums, this gorgeous oil blend can also help dads to find that 15 minutes of peace and relaxation which in turn helps with stress management and to prevent PND.

Routine in the Womb is our own branded aromatherapy blend made especially to help you find 15 minutes of relaxation in a stressful world.

Crystals

Blue Chalcedony

Hopefully mum will already have her Rose Quartz next to the bed that dad can benefit from too, so for dad this wonderful blue stone is all about nurturing their bond with baby whilst also giving them a much-needed voice to express any worries or anything important to them.

I find most dads don't want to carry crystals around and so placing next to your bed is just as good!

Meditation

Dad's Army
Meditation is just as important for dad as it is for mum as managing their own stress levels helps to reduce the risk of PND whilst supporting them on this journey too. Don't forget you need time in nature too so if you can get out and meditate, even just in the garden for 15 minutes, it will boost the power of your meditation.

Our Dad's Army meditation has been specially written to support the oil blend and boost your 15 minutes of relaxation.

Heka Balancing

Emotional Balance
One of the things dads say to me is 'I just don't have enough energy for it all' and so taking some time to replenish that energy through balancing is a must for new dads – it will also help find some emotional balance in those crazy first weeks!

Focusing on some emotional balance and stress release during heka sessions will support this important part of your journey.

The Relaxed Dad CHECKLIST

- ✓ You are on this journey together so enjoy every step, learn everything too and make choices together
- ✓ You matter to your baby. You can sing to your baby, read to your baby and bond with your baby. Just have fun, they won't be judging!
- ✓ Talking about your worries and concerns is not a sign of weakness, it is the sign of a Super Hero dad
- ✓ Take care of you! You can't take care of the family if you don't take care of you too
- ✓ You have your Dad's Army Toolkit and you're not afraid to use it

Chapter Thirteen
Safety First

babyopathy
Relaxed Mum, Contented Baby!

Safety First

Safety is not something that parents often think about with a newborn baby. However, there are lots of incidents that happen that could easily be avoided if only someone pointed them out. In addition, rather than thinking about 'safety', a lot of parents have other fears and concerns and so I thought I would talk a little about these too.

Parents' fears

For most parents I have spoken to over the years when they have brought their newborn baby home, their biggest fears are: how will I know...?

- *If they are hungry*
- *If they have fed enough*
- *When should they sleep*
- *How do I change their nappy*
- *How do I bath my baby*

You would be surprised how many new parents, especially dads, worry about these things. To be honest, with all of these things you can't really go wrong, your baby will soon tell you if they are hungry or tired, and until you get to know just what each of the cries mean you can try them all, change the nappy, offer a feed and if all that fails, get them to sleep! The only piece of critical advice when bathing your baby, hold on tight as wet babies are slippery babies!

Once you get over these first fears and realise it will all just happen you soon replace them with others, so don't worry (yes, said with tongue in cheek…!).

Seriously though, fears seem to grow as your baby grows and two of the biggest I think parents always have in the back of their minds are meningitis and cot death.

Cases of cot death or Sudden Infant Death Syndrome (SIDS) have thankfully reduced greatly over the years due to research and sound advice when putting your baby to sleep: (from www.nhs.uk)

- ✿ *Place your baby on their back to sleep, in a cot in the room with you*
- ✿ *Do not smoke during your pregnancy or let anyone smoke in the same room as your baby*
- ✿ *Do not share a bed with your baby if you or your partner smoke or take drugs or have been drinking alcohol*
- ✿ *Never sleep with your baby on a sofa or armchair*
- ✿ *Don't let your baby get too hot or too cold*
- ✿ *Keep your baby's head uncovered; their blanket should be tucked in no higher than their shoulders*
- ✿ *Place your baby in the 'feet to foot' position (with their feet touching the end of the cot or pram)*
- ✿ *If possible, breastfeed your baby*

I would like to say straight away in response to the above, do not think that if you don't breastfeed you will be putting your baby at risk, it is the standard NHS advice on most things.

However, with regards to all of the other advice, it is sound advice to follow and not just to prevent SIDS. You should **never** sleep with your baby on a sofa or armchair as there is a risk you could roll on to your baby. It also never hurts to remind babysitters and grandparents etc. of this too!

The other advice regarding not sharing a bed with your baby if you have been drinking etc. I would extend to never sleep with your baby in your bed. If you are breastfeeding and lay the baby on the bed whilst feeding this is fine, but when they have finished, place them back in their cot. First of all it will help to establish a better routine but also I remember just how exhausted I felt with my babies and falling into a deep sleep even for just a few minutes could be catastrophic if you roll on your baby.

If you are that tired and your baby won't sleep it is better that they cry in their cot for a while than they fall asleep on you and you roll on them.

Now a few words on meningitis: babies will have many temperatures during their lifetime but there are other symptoms associated with meningitis and septicaemia and a baby may show only some or many of them: (from www.meningitis.org)

- ✿ *Fever and/or vomiting*
- ✿ *Severe headache*
- ✿ *Limb/joint/muscle pain*
- ✿ *Cold hands/feet and shivering*
- ✿ *Pale or mottled skin*
- ✿ *Breathing fast or breathless*
- ✿ *Stiff neck*
- ✿ *Dislike of bright lights*
- ✿ *Very sleepy/vacant/difficult to wake*
- ✿ *Confused/delirious*
- ✿ *Seizures*
- ✿ *Rash (anywhere on the body)*

Generally, with the rash the test that is recommended is to press a clear glass over the spots or rash and if it does not disappear seek medical attention immediately. However, in some circumstances this is not the case and if you are at all worried, speak to your GP.

Also with babies under three months old they may not always have a fever but will have some or all of the other symptoms.

It is always important to be vigilant but not panic; with anything that seems out of the ordinary with your baby, stop, take a deep breath and think whether there is an explanation for your concern. If you are still concerned, or that nagging 'instinct' just won't go away then seek advice.

First Aid

First aid for babies is almost an entire book on its own and I am not an expert so the best piece of advice I can give any pregnant mum and her partner is to take a Paediatric First Aid course. They are not (or should not be) expensive but are invaluable when it comes to the well-being of your baby. As you will see from the section on babysitters, I recommend the course for them and grandparents too.

There are, however, a couple of aromatherapy and other 'must have' remedies when it comes to first aid:

Sunburn

Sponge with cold (not iced just cold tap) water until the skin is thoroughly cooled. Then mix three drops of lavender per 5ml of grapeseed oil (olive oil is OK if need be) and let it soak on the sunburnt area. If the sunburn is blistering seek medical attention and do not use oil.

Other burns and scalds

Most importantly cool the affected area. Do this by running under cold water or sit in a cold bath and sponge for at least 10 minutes. Gently pat the skin dry with a non-fluffy, preferably cotton fabric and then apply some neat lavender oil directly on to the affected area.

IMPORTANT NOTE: with 2nd or 3rd degree burns and any sign of blistering from a burn apply a cotton dressing to protect the affected area and seek urgent medical attention. Do NOT use oil or any fluffy fabric or cotton wool.

Wasp stings

For a wasp sting the best thing to put on it immediately is vinegar (cider vinegar is best); you can also put on a drop of lavender or tea tree oil to prevent infection.

Bee and ant stings

Bee stings are different from wasp stings and first of all it is likely you will need to remove the sting, but make sure you do this from the bottom of the sting closest to the skin otherwise you could leave part of it behind that becomes very hard to remove; using tweezers is best if you have them to hand.

Once the sting is removed, or just directly for ant stings, mix a teaspoon of bicarbonate of soda with some distilled water (you can put some in a little dark glass bottle in your first aid kit ready to mix up when needed) into a paste and apply on the sting.

Eczema

Although not a first aid issue, it can be extremely frustrating and flare up unexpectedly so if you need to try something that may give a quick relief use one drop of chamomile oil in five teaspoons of grapeseed oil and massage into affected area.

If you have some raw oats then put a tablespoon into a muslin bag and tie it underneath the bath tap (remove before putting baby in) when it's running to create a milky/cloudy-looking bath and then sponge over the affected areas. The water should be lukewarm when sponging.

Coughs and colds

If your baby has a cough or cold then you can add a drop of eucalyptus oil to the chamomile oil in your oil burner to help with decongestion. Raise their mattress by putting a pillow under it (not directly under the baby) so that it helps with natural mucus drainage. Depending on their age and whether they are weaned, avoid potatoes, dairy and bread (if breastfeeding it is worth you abstaining for a while too).

Asthma

If your baby has been diagnosed with asthma you can still use chamomile oil but just three drops on a tissue in the room rather than in a vaporiser or burner.

To promote milk flow

Definitely not a first aid matter but I thought it still worth a mention! Put three drops of lemongrass oil into 5ml of grapeseed oil and massage directly into the breast.

Engorgement

This can be extremely painful for mum and so anything you can do to help is welcome. The old wives' tale of putting cuts into cabbage leaves and putting directly on to your breast is still one to try but I also recommend either geranium or peppermint oil on a cold compress on your breasts is best.

One last remedy – for morning sickness

I have already mentioned a few things you can try but this is one to try before bed. One teaspoon of freshly grated ginger, ½ lemon juice squeezed into the cup and one teaspoon of honey, fill the cup with boiling water, mix thoroughly and sip before you sleep. To be honest it can be used at any time of the day and is great for colds too when you are pregnant (or not) and want to avoid paracetamol.

Baby's room

Looking around department stores and the numerous baby shows and magazines, decorating a baby's room is BIG business! There are so many accessories to decorate your baby's cot or room with but not all of them are suitable. There are a few basic rules to think about:

- ❀ *Do not use anything around your baby's cot (e.g. cot bumpers); your baby needs airflow to avoid getting too hot (remember the SIDS advice)*
- ❀ *Do not place anything around your baby's cot that could fall in, or as they grow be pulled in*
- ❀ *Window blinds: always ensure the pull cords are tied up out of reach; babies and young children have died from entanglement in cords*
- ❀ *Lights and other electronic devices: always ensure electrical leads are out of reach, cannot be pulled or become tangled in*

❧ *Electric sockets: always cover empty sockets and do not place a cot next to a socket that has something plugged in, even young babies are inquisitive*

When it comes to the colour of your baby's room I generally bow to the expertise of June McLeod and you can see her recommendations in her book *Colours of the Soul*. The colour you choose though should be calming and soothing as their room will be for sleeping and *not* for playing. My recommendations can be found on the website as they blend with our recommended natural imagery.

As your baby's eyesight develops they begin to see contrasting colours first and this becomes a source of stimulation so they are best avoided in your baby's bedroom. Complement your chosen background colour with complementary muted colours and natural imagery such as those I have shown you in the earlier chapters so that your baby is given a sense of security and well-being.

A source of music is a must as is, in my opinion, an aromatherapy oil burner, Himalayan salt lamp and finally a blackout blind. During the day, natural sunlight is essential to your baby but at night we want them to sleep, even in the summer months, so invest in a blackout blind. As for the oils to use in your baby's bedroom the only ones I would recommend are lavender during their first three months and then our Sleep Time blend, and they can be diffused for 10 minutes just before your baby is due to go to bed to create a sensory environment, not a continual smell all night.

Finally, and most importantly, have fun creating your baby's very own sensory oasis!

There's a baby in the house

It may sound silly because your baby isn't crawling or walking yet but you do need to think about safety when you have a baby in the house.

We have covered your baby's room but there are other areas you need to think about. I know some may seem like common sense but these have been causes of accidents:

Hot drinks	Do not drink hot drinks whilst holding a baby or pass over someone holding a baby – even a drop can scald. Always place out of reach of a baby.
Baby chairs *(bouncers)*	Only place on the floor – never on a higher surface that it can fall from. Do not place under objects that could fall; a young baby died when a TV fell from a cupboard on to their baby chair.
Baby carriers	There are so many styles of baby carriers on the market but the ones that fill me with horror sometimes are the front carrying ones. I have seen so many babies strapped into these things incorrectly, straps around the baby's throat, babies hanging out one side which must be causing discomfort, and even a newborn's head allowed to thrash around and hang back at an alarming angle. PLEASE look at the position your baby is in whatever type of carrier you use.
Stairs	Always try to carry your baby securely with one arm so you keep one hand on the banister (I fell down the stairs carrying my baby and can tell you how scary it is). Always use stair gates, falls are one of the biggest reasons for visiting Accident & Emergency. Do not leave things on the stairs that can cause you to trip.
Pets	NEVER leave your baby in a room with a pet; they can lie on your baby causing suffocation or cause harm through biting or scratching. Even the most docile, seemingly protective animal can behave unexpectedly, especially if your baby cries.

This list is by no means exhaustive, there are endless lists of things you should do to child-proof your home especially the bathroom and kitchen, but I wanted to get you to think about some of the more common sense things that don't always get mentioned. One of the best places to find advice on baby safety in the home is www. nhs.uk and search for 'safety for babies'.

As baby moves

As your baby gets older and starts to move there are other safety points to think about and believe it or not we continually see bumps, bruises and even more serious injuries coming into nursery from these easily prevented safety points:

Sitting up	This is a crucial skill for your baby to learn but can result in lots of bumps and bruises until they gain control. Always place cushions around your baby and ensure there are no sharp or hard objects to fall against, including furniture. Rolling is a common precursor to sitting and is the first thing they learn and surprise you with especially when baby falls over from a sitting position. So never leave your baby on any surface other than the floor once they have started to move – they can roll fast!
Crawling	Once a baby is mobile anything in arm's reach is fair game and whilst I didn't move everything (learning 'no' is important) it is best to move anything that can be swallowed, a choking hazard or is sharp etc. Safety gates on the stairs are recommended from now.
Standing up	As with crawling, anything your baby can now reach is a toy to them so the same rules apply. A crucial part of standing up is pulling themselves up on things so ensure anything that is in reach is suitable for them to do that with and will not topple over on them.
Walking	Once a baby walks they go from one or two steps to running very quickly. Always hold your baby's hand when you are outside the home (especially by roads or cars in car parks) and they are walking, there are plenty of safe places they can run free. Big windows such as patio doors are a huge hazard to walking/running babies and children, so do what my mum did for my grandchildren: stick family photos or other pictures on them so your baby can see it is a barrier.

Again, it is impossible to list all of the hazards to your baby as every home is different but the aim is to make you think.

Do's and don'ts

It is very hard when writing a book deciding just how much to put in, especially when you want to be different from all the other books out there. I know some of the things I have covered, particularly in this safety section, are mentioned in many places: other books, magazines and websites etc. However, I want this book to be full of all the things I still see parents do that without realising can cause harm and can be prevented and so here are some other do's and don'ts when it comes to your baby.

Rough and tumble

Whilst I think sometimes we wrap our children up in cotton wool we also have to be careful that we aren't taking things too far without realising. One of the things you need to avoid is throwing your baby up in the air. It is something I don't see so much now thankfully but it can put too much strain on your baby's neck, and if for whatever reason you drop them, it can cause damage and even Shaken Baby Syndrome.

Picking up baby by their arms

This is something that absolutely infuriates me! Worse than smacking a child is grabbing or dragging (yes, sadly I have seen it) a baby or young child up by their arms or gripping their arms at their shoulders (usually whilst shouting too). It can cause injuries to their wrists, hands or shoulders, even a dislocation. It might not be intentional but it is just as painful for your baby.

Cold weather

Everyone, not only babies, loses heat through their head, hands and feet; you buy hats, scarves and gloves for yourself so please do the same for your baby. I have seen babies in snow suits but then with no shoes/bootees or hat, completely defeating the objective.

Also, baby's skin is very sensitive and so the cold and wind can cause chapped skin especially on their cheeks, so protect it with a suitable moisturiser.

Hot weather

Just as with cold weather, a baby will feel the effects of the heat through their head and so a sun hat is a must. One of the things that amazes me every time I see it is a parent wearing sunglasses and sometimes a sun hat, protecting themselves, but then pushing their baby, facing forward, exposed to the full sun. A sunshade or parasol is a must, it can prevent your baby getting overheated and even sunburn. Most importantly do not use blankets, muslins or any other material to cover over the pram; it can cause the temperature within the pram to rise to a high level putting your baby at risk from heat stroke.

Don't forget your baby will need extra fluids (cooled boiled water) when it is particularly hot too!

Prams and older children

Did you know prams are actually climbing frames for older children? As well as your baby possibly falling out when it is pulled over, your older child can sustain a nasty injury if they fall from the pram or the pram falls on them.

Older children

Older children may love their new baby brother or sister but they may just seem like a life-size doll to them. I will never forget a story told to me by the Under Eights Officer from Social Services that registered my first nursery. She had two older children already when her third was born. She needed to use the bathroom and put the new baby in the pram whilst her older two were occupied playing. As she sat on the loo she heard the baby cry but then stop; the next thing she saw was her oldest child, about five at the time, walk into the bathroom saying, 'It's OK Mummy, I have the baby.' Unfortunately, she was carrying the baby how she carries her dolls, her arm around their neck! Needless to say, she told me she didn't even have a chance to pull up her pants before retrieving the baby from her oldest child. The moral of this story: never leave your baby with an older child.

It's YOUR baby

I remember a story someone told me once about someone who picked up their baby. The person was wearing an old coat that smelled of smoke and was covered in dog hair and they were holding their beautifully clean newborn baby against it. For whatever reason, they didn't feel able to say anything but they should have. Remember, it is YOUR baby and everyone should ask before they pick them up and you have the right to say no.

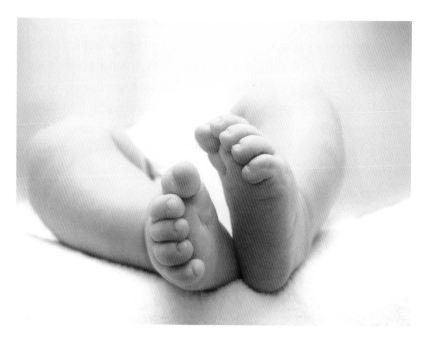

Chapter Fourteen
Babyopathy For Life

Relaxed Mum, Contented Baby!

Babyopathy For Life

So, you're almost ready to graduate and get your Babyopathy Relaxed Mum status – have you ordered your Babyopathy Super Hero t-shirt yet? You must realise by now that I'm also a huge Marvel fan as well as Disney!

Let's just go through the main checklist:

✓ **You took care of you through every stage and always do –** *you can't take the best care of baby if you don't take care of you*

✓ **You listen to your own instincts and common sense and not the latest trend/social media gossip – you are what is best for you and your baby and never feel pressured to do something or be like somebody else**

✓ **Baby has you, not technology! –** *your baby needs you to be interacting with them and not your phone – that way they don't need expensive plastic substitute toys either!*

Your baby is a blank canvas:

✿ *They do not know hatred*

✿ *They do not know racism or discrimination*

✿ *They do not know how to be judgmental or hurtful*

SO, DON'T TEACH THEM HOW TO BE!

Your baby, however, also does not know:

- ✿ *Compassion*
- ✿ *Effective communication*
- ✿ *Patience and manners*
- ✿ *Respect*

THEY WILL LEARN THIS BY WATCHING YOU!

So, let them learn to be an amazing Super Hero by watching you be one too!

You and your baby lead a Babyopathy life!

– you spend time in nature, you nurture your senses and you enjoy life together doing what is best for you and your family!

It's that simple! Now my fully fledged Babyopathy Super Heroes, go fly with that gorgeous and unique in every way Babyopathy Baby and remember, relaxed mum, contented baby!

A DISCLAIMER REMINDER – if you are unable to do any of the above, if you choose not to do any of the above or you simply missed out on doing any of the above, it does not make you a bad parent or exclude you from being a relaxed mum or a Super Hero, as let's face it, they (Super Heroes) come in all shapes and sizes and with different super powers. I am simply bringing you all of the information (or as much as possible) together in one place, to help you make informed choices for both your own well-being and that of your baby. If you don't like any of the above or don't agree with it, you don't need to troll me – just don't do it! Plus, I have always loved the Super Hero movies (especially *The Incredibles*!) – who doesn't want to be a Super Hero!

But remember, we are always here if you need us:

Website: **www.babyopathy.com**
Facebook: **www.facebook.com/babyopathy**
www.facebook.com/routineinthewomb
Twitter: **www.twitter.com/babyopathy**
Instagram: **www.instagram.com/babyopathy**

References and Useful Contacts

Laura Sharman B.Ost
Cranial Osteopath
Ware Osteopathy Clinic
www.wareosteopathyclinic.co.uk

Natasha Crowe
Psychotherapist, Counsellor & Easy-Birthing Practitioner
www.warehypnotherapy.com

June McLeod
Colour Psychologist
www.colourpsychologytoday.com

Shirley O'Donoghue
Lucis College
www.lucisgroup.com

Debbie Best
Nutritionist
www.best-nutrition.co.uk

Dr Calvin J Hobel
OB/GYN- Maternal Foetal Medicine
Cedars-Sinai Hospital, Los Angeles
The current research of Calvin J Hobel MD focuses on the role of maternal behaviours, the environment and the genetic risk of both pre-term birth and poor foetal growth. The research laboratory is studying the role of stress hormones on the risk of pre-term birth and the search for resilience factors that may decrease the risk of pre-term birth. Most recently, the research group is assessing vitamin D deficiency during pregnancy and its role in infection as a cause of pre-term birth and also its role in insulin resistance in diabetic pregnancies.

Dr Pathik Wadhwa
Assistant Professor of Behavioural Science, Obstetrics and Gynaecology
University of Kentucky College of Medicine, USA

Edwin O Wilson
University of Harvard, USA

Stephen R Kellert
Tweedy Ordway Professor Emeritus of Social Ecology
Yale University, USA
www.stephenrkellert.net

Dr Dimitri Christakis
Director of Seattle Children's Research Institute for Child Health, Behaviour and Development and Professor of Paediatrics
University of Washington School of Medicine

PANDAS
www.pandasfoundation.org.uk

or call their Helpline on **0843 28 98 401**
Meningitis Research Foundation
www.meningitis.org

About the Author

Angela owned and operated children's nurseries for over 25 years – opening her first in 1993 at the age of 21 – and was named in the Top 10 most influential people in Childcare by *NMT Magazine* in 2017 before finally selling the nurseries in 2018.

As a mum, after neither of her children slept through the night for their first three years, Angela decided to research deeper into child development and everything that can nurture or have an adverse effect on it. This research quickly took the route of sensory stimulation, and the first programme called Natural Care was introduced into her Angels at Play nurseries in 2000. Angela's children are now 19 and 22 years old and she is delighted to also now be a grandmother, her daughter experiencing the full benefits of Babyopathy and the birthing programme.

The research did not stop there though, and from using her own natural imagery within the nurseries, Angela began researching the impact of the natural world on development and came across the biophilia hypothesis which is also now incorporated into her newly named Nascuropathy Programme and Babyopathy (for pregnancy and under one-year-olds). Babyopathy was featured in *Mother & Baby* magazine as 'the New Routine for 2017'.

REEDS MARINE ENGINEERING AND TECHNOLOGY SERIES